"The apostle Peter tells us to always be ready to answer anyone who asks for a reason for the hope we have (1 Pet. 3:15). Being ready doesn't have to be intimidating. Chip Ingram has presented a straightforward case for why he believes. This book will help strengthen your own belief and give you resources for communicating it to others."

Jim Daly, president of Focus on the Family

"This is a keeper—a classic! Take it home and put it with your Bible. After reading God's Word (His Word must have priority), read a chapter of *Why I Believe* with a pen! You will learn so much that will help you encounter the culture in a powerful way. In fact, buy a few extra copies because you will want others to have this book. It's a gift of high value—a great tool for the gospel! Thanks, beloved brother, for equipping us for the work of ministry so, like the apostle Paul, we can move into our cities and reason from the Word!"

Kay Arthur, cofounder of Precept Ministries International

"Chip Ingram has a way of taking complex and intimidating material and making it accessible and applicable to everyone. That's the reason I didn't just pick up one copy of *Why I Believe* to add to the apologetics section of my bookshelf, but why I ordered boxes of this book. As a pastor, I will be handing it out for years to come."

Kyle Idleman, pastor; author of *Grace Is Greater*

"*Why I Believe* tackles some of the toughest questions of our day. Through both research and personal stories, Chip shares why he went from a full-blown skeptic to a Christian. Whether you are a believer or a skeptic, you will be greatly encouraged and challenged by the stories and evidence in this book."

Sean McDowell, PhD, author, speaker, professor

"Chip Ingram has given us a fantastic guide for not only knowing what we believe but for owning, understanding, and defending those beliefs. His careful attention to doubts and questions will help Christians dive deeper into their faith and live it out more fully. Read, study, and share this book."

Andy Stanley, senior pastor of North Point Ministries

"I love this book! In the introduction to *Why I Believe*, Chip Ingram says, 'I'm not an expert apologist.' I respectfully disagree. I think this is one of the most practical, straightforward, factual, and best books I have ever read on the validity of our Christian faith. Chip is a master at taking a complicated topic and making it totally understandable. Read this book, then pass it on to your family and friends."

Jim Burns, PhD, president of HomeWord; author of *Creating an Intimate Marriage* and *Confident Parenting*

"We all need straight answers to the questions we ask about God, faith, and the Bible. Chip Ingram helps us to get our hearts and minds around the most important issues we face and offers authentic and transparent answers. If you want to clarify and fortify your faith, this book is for you."

Jack Graham, pastor of Prestonwood Baptist Church, Plano, TX

"Chip Ingram distills a lifetime of study into a volume that will help any believer fully follow Christ. I wish I had this book available when I was a new Christian. It's written in Chip's honest, authentic style. My prediction is that you will be dog-earring and highlighting this book for a long time. And you will use the content to lead others to faith."

Chris Fabry, novelist; host of Chris Fabry Live on Moody Radio

"Every follower of Christ rubs shoulders with the skeptical, the curious, and the antagonistic each day. Yet, despite the ample opportunity provided, believers often shun the chance to open their mouths to defend the faith. Why the stifling silence? They feel ill-equipped to tackle the tough questions lobbed their way. Ingram seeks to remove such excuses. *Why I Believe* provides practical help to enable every Christian to cogently explain what they believe. Keep this book within arm's reach at all times."

Paul Nyquist, president of Moody Bible Institute

"Chip Ingram is both a student and teacher of God's Word. After reading Chip's practical treatment on the distinctives of the faith, *my own* biblical beliefs were strengthened. Yours will be too."

Dave Stone, pastor of Southeast Christian Church, Louisville, KY

"Chip Ingram is a passionate pastor-teacher who models a commitment to Scripture and writes to help others get there as well. This new book, *Why I Believe*, is a welcome text that is well-written and well-reasoned for a new generation struggling to ground their faith in the untarnished truth of the Bible."

Mark L. Bailey, president of Dallas Theological Seminary

"If you're a cynic or skeptic about Christianity, you will relate to Chip's book. He's been there. If you don't know much about the Bible, this book is perfect for you in understanding basic insight to see how faith in God just makes sense."

Bryant Wright, senior pastor of
Johnson Ferry Baptist Church, Marietta, GA

"In a time of confusion and shared ignorance in Western culture, Chip Ingram has given us a masterpiece and explanation that the Christian faith is easily reasoned and defended. You should not only read this book but give it away to every genuine inquirer."

Michael Youssef, PhD, executive president of Leading the Way

"It's the nagging questions about God, His Word, and His ways that often inhibit our passionate pursuit of Him. My friend Chip Ingram helps us navigate the tough questions with a clear and convincing conversation that will help us settle our doubts and stimulate our faith."

Dr. Joseph M. Stowell, president of
Cornerstone University, Grand Rapids, MI

"The apostle Peter tells us to always be ready to make a defense for the hope that is in us. Chip has made our task a lot easier by writing, *Why I Believe*. It is unique in that it's brief, concise, and simple, yet at the same time, thorough. Whether you read it to defend your own faith or do so to investigate the Christian faith for yourself, *Why I Believe* is a must-read for all."

Randy Pope, pastor of Perimeter Church, Johns Creek, GA

"My friend Chip Ingram has a gift for simplifying the complex truths of Christianity. Whether you're seeking to bolster your faith or to explore the possibility of having faith, you will find meaningful answers in *Why I Believe*. Profound and practical, *Why I Believe* answers our common questions about the Christian faith."

John S. Dickerson, Livingston Award for Young Journalists recipient; bestselling author of *The Great Evangelical Recession*

"With his usual clarity and practical skills, my friend Chip Ingram has crafted a simple but compelling approach to several of the great questions about the faith. He puts the cookies on a low enough shelf to be accessible to all, but does so without distorting or dumbing down the critical issues. I welcome this winsome and engaging resource."

Dr. Kenneth Boa, writer and speaker, Reflections Ministries, Atlanta, GA

"*Why I Believe* is a tremendous resource for an era when basic tenets of Christianity are being called into question. Chip Ingram addresses challenging questions and important issues in Christian apologetics in a characteristically clear, concise, approachable manner. This is a book for believers, skeptics, searchers, apologists, students, pastors, and everyone in between."

Barry H. Corey, president of Biola University; author of *Love Kindness: Discover the Power of a Forgotten Christian Virtue*

WHY I
BELIEVE

WHY I BELIEVE

Straight Answers to
Honest Questions about God,
the Bible, and Christianity

CHIP INGRAM

BakerBooks
a division of Baker Publishing Group
Grand Rapids, Michigan

© 2017 by Chip Ingram

Published by Baker Books
a division of Baker Publishing Group
PO Box 6287, Grand Rapids, MI 49516-6287
www.bakerbooks.com

Printed in the United States of America

Library of Congress Cataloging-in-Publication Data
Names: Ingram, Chip, 1954– author.
Title: Why I believe : straight answers to honest questions about God, the Bible, and
    Christianity / Chip Ingram.
Description: Grand Rapids, MI : Baker Books, a division of Baker Publishing
    Group, 2017. | Includes bibliographical references.
Identifiers: LCCN 2017020773| ISBN 9780801073120 (cloth) | ISBN 9780801074387
    (pbk.)
Subjects: LCSH: Apologetics.
Classification: LCC BT1103 .I54 2017 | DDC 239—dc23
LC record available at https://lccn.loc.gov/2017020773

17 18 19 20 21 22 23   7 6 5 4 3 2 1

Contents

Introduction

I didn't grow up as a follower of Christ and my experience with organized religion was negative. As a kid, I got the distinct impression that no one actually believed what they were telling me but felt children needed to hear stories about Jesus in order to keep them out of trouble. It was obvious to me that the adults who espoused the religious platitudes and rituals that I was expected to follow didn't live by them themselves. There was no expectation that the truth of the Word of God would have any impact on how we would live our lives.

The hypocrisy and lack of authenticity hardened my heart, and I became a full-blown skeptic prior to my sixteenth birthday. My inward attitudes toward church, organized religion, and God were suspect at best and highly negative at worst. I somehow intuitively concluded that God, Santa Claus, the Easter Bunny, and the Tooth Fairy were all adult fabrications to keep children in the dark and pacify their hard questions until they could come of age and discover the answers for themselves.

I share this important part of my early years because it created an attitude and a perspective that I've never lost. I'm a skeptic at heart. I'm not necessarily proud of that, but I simply don't believe what's presented at face value. My tendency is to assume there is an ulterior motive. I am always looking for the other side of the story, and wonder what someone is hiding from me until I can prove differently.

Immediately following high school, our great God met my skepticism with evidence that was overwhelming. At this stage of my life, it wasn't intellectual evidence but relational authenticity and love. God brought me into contact with a group of athletes whom I deeply respected. I had never read the Bible despite my church experience, and I had never heard it communicated practically and relevantly. In 1972, at a Fellowship of Christian Athletes weeklong camp, I both heard and saw the gospel for the first time.

I responded by faith to the invitation of Revelation 3:20 by inviting Jesus to come into my life and trusting Him for the forgiveness of my sins. The decision was mine. No one told me what to do. No lists of rules or rituals were given to me to follow. I had a new relationship with God that was personal, and I learned that He speaks to me through His Word.

I went home with the Bible that I was now beginning to understand and with a peace that I couldn't understand. I had an appetite for the Scriptures that was unexplainable. Within a few weeks, I saw dramatic changes in my desires and my behavior.

The change that first year was so dramatic that my father asked me what had happened to me. My priorities changed.

My insecurities and arrogance had surfaced and were softened with peace and confidence in Christ. I went to a secular school on a basketball scholarship where I met a bricklayer trained by the Navigators. By the time I graduated, his Bible study of three people (including me) had mushroomed to over 250 students, and countless others were impacted as God birthed a Christian movement on campus.

If this sounds a bit like a cheesy Christian movie, in many ways it was . . . that is, until just before graduation. Dr. P., the head of our department, asked me a question that exposed every skeptical bone in my body.

I can remember that day like it was yesterday. I can still picture the sun bouncing off the windows of the ivy-covered brick building outside of Dr. P.'s office as we had a conversation that would change the course of my life. He was a brilliant professor and the department chair. He liked me and I liked him. I may not have been the smartest in the department, but I got straight A's in my major and had a passion to learn. He watched my life for four years and was well aware of my love and passion for Christ.

As we talked outside his office, I had the sense that he had waited until I finished all my classes and was graduating with honors before he asked me this question:

"Chip, how can someone as well-educated and intellectually astute as you appear to be, really believe in a literal Jesus and all this born-again stuff?"

His tone was not harsh or attacking. It actually was more pastoral, born out of a heart of concern and disappointment that one of his favorite students could potentially be throwing away his future, along with his brains, to blindly follow an ancient book and a mythical figure named Jesus.

I deeply respected Dr. P., and I did not take his question lightly. It cast a series of doubts deep down in my heart. Could all this be simply an emotional experience in my formative college years? Could I really answer the tough questions he began to ask about why I believed in Jesus, the Bible, creation, and life after death? Was I willing to throw my brains in the trash to be a follower of Christ? Was my faith real?

That conversation began a journey that is coming to a climax in this book. I made a number of very specific decisions that day:

1. I would not throw my brains in the trash to be a follower of Christ. If my faith was true, it must hold up under intellectual, philosophical, and historical scrutiny.
2. I could not deny the life-changing experience that Jesus had made in my life, and so I would not be intellectually intimidated into giving up my faith simply because those I respected in academia belittled it.
3. I would fully commit myself to discover the answers to those hard questions, if they existed, and let the consequences of my research and study direct my future.

It has been a long and sometimes difficult journey. I have read and researched multiple sides of these important issues, and my skeptical background has helped me to be objective. I knew that I could not follow Jesus if there were not real answers to the very deep questions that had to be addressed.

This book is aptly titled—*Why I Believe*. I am not an expert apologist and I do not have PhDs in multiple areas of research like some of our best Christian apologists. I'm so grateful for them and I've carefully studied their work along with those who disagree with them. My aim is to synthesize the best research and thinking in a way that makes it easy to understand and practical to apply.

This book is designed to provide well-researched and practical guidelines for us ordinary people to fully understand the intellectual and historical basis for our faith, and to talk intelligently and confidently with our friends, family, and coworkers over a cup of coffee about why we believe. Layout and design will allow you to grasp the material quickly and the endnotes will allow you to go to other resources for more specific information.

I have spent most of my ministry teaching in parts of the country where people have little or no biblical background but are very intellectually astute. I have learned and become fully convinced that I do not have to throw my brains in the trash to be a fully devoted follower of the historic Jesus, who died to pay for our sins, who rose from the dead, who believed the Scriptures to be the very Word of God, and who promised to come again to execute justice and make all things new.

So I want to invite you to go on a journey with me. I want to share with you what I have learned and answer the question my professor asked all those years ago. I want you to discover firsthand that there is substantial and reasonable evidence for our faith in the Jesus of the Bible. My faith in God and my life as a Christ follower is not belief "in spite of the lack of evidence," as some have claimed. Quite the contrary, my faith is built on an historical, intellectual, scientific, and philosophical foundation that answers life's biggest questions and stands up to its harshest critics.

Join me now as we prepare our hearts and minds to respond to the admonition of the Lord Jesus through the apostle Peter:

> But in your hearts revere Christ as Lord. Always be prepared to give an answer to everyone who asks you to give the reason for the hope that you have. But do this with gentleness and respect, keeping a clear conscience, so that those who speak maliciously against your good behavior in Christ may be ashamed of their slander. (1 Pet. 3:15–16)

1

Why I Believe
in the Resurrection

Jesus said to her, "I am the resurrection and the life. The one who believes in me will live, even though they die; and whoever lives by believing in me will never die. Do you believe this?"

John 11:25–26

As we begin our journey together to answer the question my professor asked me, there's one thing that very good atheists and very good Christians have in common. The central issue for these diametrically opposed groups is the resurrection of Jesus Christ. It's where we must begin. Either Jesus rose from the dead, or He's just another religious teacher and you should go to the salad bar of religion and pick the one you like. But if He really rose from the dead, if He's actually alive right now, and if we worship a living Savior and His resurrection power actually lives inside our mortal bodies . . . then that is a whole different story.

Life after death is a timeless cultural preoccupation. The ability to beat death and have a second chance at life sounds like a popular movie plot. From comic book heroes to zombie outbreaks and everything in between, our culture seems to be obsessed with the idea of "coming back from the dead." We binge-watch TV shows on the topic and search online for first-person accounts of what it's like to come back to life after being pronounced clinically dead. Let me tell you, there is one "coming back from the dead" story that dramatically stands apart from all the rest. It offers real hope to all of humanity.

Listen to what the apostle Paul writes to the Corinthians:

> If there is no resurrection of the dead, then not even Christ has been raised. And if Christ has not been raised, our preaching is useless and so is your faith. More than that, we are then found to be false witnesses about God, for we have testified about God that he raised Christ from the dead. But he did not raise him if in fact the dead are not raised. For if the dead are not raised, then Christ has not been raised either. And if Christ has not been raised, your faith is futile; you are still in your sins. Then those also who have fallen asleep in Christ are lost. If only for this life we have hope in Christ, we are of all people most to be pitied. (1 Cor. 15:13–19)

According to the apostle Paul, if the bodily resurrection of Jesus Christ isn't true, Christianity is a hoax, and it's a bad one, and none of it is true.

Despite the centuries of skepticism and criticism, the truth remains that the resurrection of Jesus Christ is central to the Christian faith. Both Christians and atheists agree that Jesus' resurrection from the dead is vital.

Prominent atheist professor of philosophy Antony Flew and Christian professor of apologetics and philosophy Gary Habermas began debating in 1985. Over the next two decades, their debates led to several books, including *Did Jesus Rise from the Dead? The Resurrection Debate*. In this book, Flew writes,

> Both Christians and atheists agree that Jesus' resurrection from the dead is vital.

> First, we [Habermas and myself] both construe *resurrection*, or the rising from the dead, in a thoroughly literal and physical way. . . .
>
> Second, we are again agreed that the question whether, in that literal understanding, Jesus did rise from the dead is of supreme theoretical and practical importance. For the knowable fact that he did, if it is indeed a knowable fact, is the best, if not the only, reason for accepting that Jesus is the God of Abraham, Isaac, and Israel.
>
> Third, we are agreed both that the identification is the defining and distinguishing characteristic of the true Christian, and that it is scarcely possible to make it without also accepting that the Resurrection did literally happen.[1]

What Flew is saying is, if Jesus rose, you have an intellectually feasible argument that everything Jesus said could be true. If he didn't, all of Christianity falls.

As we continue our journey together in this chapter and the next, I want to share seven reasons why I personally believe in the Jesus of the Bible as an actual historical figure who literally died and was raised from the dead.

Reason #1: The Historicity of Jesus of Nazareth

Did Jesus of Nazareth really exist as a human being? Was He created by believers in an attempt to support their cause and then added to history books based on thousands of years of hearsay? Is there any record of His life in other writings, not just the Bible? How can I know for sure that He is not myth or legend like King Arthur, Zeus, or the Titans?

The written evidence for the historicity of Jesus of Nazareth is extremely strong. There are over twenty-five thousand New Testament documents that authenticate the reality of Jesus Christ. There is more evidence supporting Jesus' life than Shakespeare, Homer, or almost any other person who has ever lived.

Non-Christian, extrabiblical sources also support the authenticity of the life of Jesus. Prominent historians include Pliny, a Roman governor and historian; Tacitus, a Roman historian living during Jesus' time; and Josephus, a Jewish historian who lived shortly after the time of Jesus. Expert historians, Christian or not, agree that Jesus was a man who lived and died in first-century Palestine. Almost all would agree that He was born near the time of Herod the Great's death, spent His childhood in Nazareth, was baptized by John the Baptist, gathered a group of disciples, taught in the villages and towns, preached the "kingdom of God," caused disturbances in the temple with His teaching, and was arrested, questioned, and executed by the order of Pontius Pilate.

Archaeological evidence exists supporting the context of Jesus' life. In 1961, a limestone block was discovered that supported the existence of Pontius Pilate. Coins have been found that were designed and minted by Pontius Pilate in 29 to 31 AD while he was the governor of Judea. In 1990, the family tomb of Caiaphas, the Jewish high priest who was involved in Jesus' trials and execution, was found. In 2012, archaeologists in Jerusalem discovered a *bulla*, a clay seal, that referenced the city of Bethlehem. Archaeologists are continually uncovering more artifacts, and I believe their findings will continue to support the historicity of Jesus. Volumes have been written with amazing examples of the archaeological support of New Testament people, places, and events. For further study in the area, I recommend *The Popular Handbook of Archaeology and the Bible* by Holden and Geisler.

Reason #2: The Character of Jesus Is Unquestioned

The second reason I believe in the resurrection of the Jesus in the New Testament is that the character of Jesus is unquestioned. At first blush, you may wonder why Jesus' character is a part of my rationale for believing in the resurrection. On my personal journey I studied the lives and movements of other religious leaders. Many of them were filled with myth and legend and divine revelations that were given to "unusual men" because of their purity and spiritual enlightenment. Yet upon further scrutiny I found historical documentation of their personal lives and history that called into question their claims of being prophets or receiving a revelation from God. Sexual immorality, greed, execution of opponents, and the like caused me to pause deeply at any of their truth claims.

So while Jesus' character does not prove His resurrection, I want you to see the significant connection of His one-of-a-kind life and the one-of-a-kind event—the resurrection. I personally find it far easier to believe that a man who claimed to be perfect (and was never challenged on the statement) rose from the dead than someone whose truth claims and stories of spiritual reality are at odds with his or her life practice.

While people challenged Jesus' claim to be the Son of God, they did not doubt His nature. All over the world and throughout time, both friend and foe alike view Jesus as a great man and moral teacher. Islam, Buddhism, and Hinduism all view Jesus positively. They do not recognize Him as the Son of God, but they see Him as a person of supreme moral character, love, and integrity. Even the New Age faith encourages a state of "Christ consciousness" and finding the "Christ within." The ideals of being a person who is good, kind, and connected to God are something to strive for. Jesus' pure actions and loving attitude toward people made it clear that He was different than anyone else.

During His lifetime, Jesus made a huge, outrageous claim—that He never sinned. Jesus says in John 8:46, "Can any of you prove me guilty of sin? If I am telling the truth, why don't you believe me?" Can you imagine going home or to work and calling everyone together to announce that you are sinless? "Hey, everybody, just want you to know that I am sinless—I have never sinned." Now, if I announced that, my kids would have volumes to say along the lines of, "Dad, you are crazy. Remember when . . ." My coworkers would probably have similar things to say.

> Jesus made a huge, outrageous claim—that He never sinned. He is never challenged on it.

But Jesus makes this claim and He is never challenged on it. All the crowds had to do was catch Him in sin one time and the entire integrity of His message and His person would be gone. The people did not call Him out as a sinner because there was nothing to accuse Him of.

Jesus' supreme moral character, love, and integrity have been affirmed by the impact they have made on world history. He has influenced history, thinking, books, law, culture, values, and even time. We mark time with BC and AD, based on the birth and death of the one person who changed the world and said, "[I've] come to seek and to save that which was lost" (Luke 19:10 NASB). We know He was an actual, historical person who lived, and we know that He was good, kind, loving, and holy.

> Jesus has influenced history, thinking, books, law, culture, values, and even time.

Reason #3: The Works of Jesus Went Unchallenged

Jesus turned water into wine at a wedding in Cana, healed the blind, the lepers, and the sick. He raised people from the dead, fed five thousand people with five loaves of bread and two fish, and performed many more miracles. The witnesses to His miracles and the religious establishment who felt threatened by Him never said, "You faked that miracle—you didn't really do it." The validity of the miracles was evident to all. While skeptics questioned the source of His power to perform miracles, it was undisputed that He did perform miracle after miracle.

In Matthew 12, Jesus heals a demon-possessed, blind, and deaf man. It was clear to everyone there that the man was healed. He was transformed—he could see and speak and was free of the demon. All the people who witnessed this miracle were astonished and asked each other if Jesus was the Messiah. "But when the Pharisees heard this, they said, 'It is only by Beelzebub, the prince of demons, that this fellow drives out demons'" (Matt. 12:24).

Over a three-year time period, Jesus performed miracles in small towns and in the populated areas of Jerusalem and Judea. The crowds swelled as word got around that Jesus healed people. The consistently growing crowds verified the authenticity of the miracles. In that day, you could meet the lady in Nain with her son, who once was dead but was brought back to life. You could go talk to the guy who was once paralyzed and see him walking around town. Or you could go talk to the leper who was once a social outcast because of his disease, now healed and part of the community.

With all of today's amazing digital editing capabilities, we are used to seeing manipulated magazine covers and computer-generated special effects in movies. We have come to expect reality to be blurred or enhanced. The agonizing decision for many people is which filter to choose before posting their pictures on their social media account. My point is that, as a culture, we are used to seeing altered images. Jesus did not use filters, computer-generated images, or special effects. Jesus' miracles were verifiable and the fact that the crowds kept growing supports the validity of His miracles.

Reason #4: The Identity of Jesus Was Confirmed

The next reason I believe in the resurrection is that the identity of Jesus was confirmed. Who is Jesus? This is one of the most important questions anyone can ask, and the answer has the power to change a person's life trajectory for eternity.

For such an important question, the variety of answers is staggering. A quick Google search pulls up pages and pages of possibilities, and the arguments between readers quickly turn personal and heated. With so many different beliefs about Jesus' identity, where do you begin to look for answers? Let's imagine you wanted to discover the identity of your new, mysterious next-door neighbor. Before you text message the contacts on your street or knock on the doors of everyone on your block, it makes sense to talk directly to the new, mysterious next-door neighbor. Go next door and find out. Get to know their name, where they are from, about their family, and what they do. This time-tested, old-school method still works. That is what we are going to do. We are going to start with what Jesus claims about Himself. Then we will look at what God says about Jesus' identity, and what many others say.

Jesus Claimed to Be God

Let's take a look at how Jesus identifies Himself throughout His life. In John 14:6, He says, "I am the way and the truth and the life. No one comes to the Father except through me."

Leading up to Jesus' crucifixion, He was taken before Caiaphas, the Jewish high priest, for a trial. In chapter 14 of Mark's account, we read that many people were testifying falsely against Jesus in front of Caiaphas, and Jesus remained silent. Finally, Caiaphas asked Jesus, "Are you the Messiah, the Son of the Blessed One?" and Jesus answered, "I am. . . . And you will see the Son of Man sitting at the right hand of the Mighty One and coming on the clouds of heaven" (vv. 61–62). Jesus' answer so offended Caiaphas that he tore his clothes and declared Jesus guilty of blasphemy, a crime punishable by death.

Why was Jesus calling Himself the "Son of Man" so shocking?

Why was Jesus calling Himself the "Son of Man" so shocking? First, Jesus answered Caiaphas by affirming that He was the Messiah, the Savior. But the title "Son of Man" has a very specific meaning. Yes, He was a human being, a son of man, but in Daniel 7 the title of "Son of Man" is given to the exalted heavenly One who will rule heaven, and that is why Jesus uses that name for Himself. He will save men from their sins, giving them eternal life, and be the exalted One who reigns forever over the kingdom of heaven.

God the Father Affirms Jesus' Identity

In Scripture, we hear the voice of God telling the world that Jesus is His Son. The first time is during His baptism and the second is on the Mount of Transfiguration.

> At that time Jesus came from Nazareth in Galilee and was baptized by John in the Jordan. Just as Jesus was coming up out of the water, he saw heaven being torn open and the Spirit descending on him like a dove. And a voice came from heaven: "You are my Son, whom I love; with you I am well-pleased." (Mark 1:9–11)

God clearly identifies Jesus as His Son. A little later in Mark 9, we read that Jesus took Peter, James, and John on a hiking trip up a high mountain. Then before their eyes His garments became radiantly, exceedingly white, and the men could see Jesus talking to Elijah and Moses.

> Then a cloud appeared and covered them, and a voice came from the cloud: "This is my Son, whom I love. Listen to him!"
> Suddenly, when they looked around, they no longer saw anyone with them except Jesus. (Mark 9:47)

God clearly identifies Jesus as His Son.

Can you imagine what it was like for His disciples, Peter, John, and James? They were living life together with Jesus. Every day was spent walking together, eating together, talking together, and together they saw Jesus heal the sick and the blind and bring the dead back to life. The disciples' account of Jesus in the Gospels further confirms His identity.

Jesus' Disciples Claimed He Is God

If you could chart the book of Mark, the first eight chapters are full of Jesus serving, healing, and teaching people to establish His credentials as the Messiah. He launched His ministry by casting out a demon, healing a paralytic, calming a storm, raising a little girl from the dead, and feeding the hungry crowd of five thousand while he taught everyone about God, the kingdom, and eternal life. Then in chapter 8, He asked His disciples, "Who do people say that I am?" And they answered, "John the Baptist, Elijah, or one of the prophets." Then Jesus asked them, "Who do you say I am?" Peter replied, "You are the Messiah" (vv. 27–29). Flesh did not reveal that to Peter; God, Jesus' Father, did. Peter knew the Old Testament. He knew all the promises and what the prophet Isaiah had said. Peter was living life alongside Jesus, listening to His teaching, watching Him heal and care for people. He was there when the blind could see, the lame walk, and the dead were raised. He heard teaching like he had never heard before, and he knew that Jesus was the Christ.

Jesus' Enemies Confirmed His Identity

Although Jesus' enemies didn't like who He claimed to be, His works went unchallenged. In John 10 we read that the Jews gathered around Jesus as He came into the temple and asked Him,

> "How long will you keep us in suspense? If you are the Messiah, tell us plainly."
>
> Jesus answered, "I did tell you, but you do not believe. The works I do in my Father's name testify about me, but you do not believe because you are not my sheep. My sheep listen to my voice; I know them, and they follow me. I give them eternal life, and they shall never perish; no one will snatch them out of my hand. My Father, who has given them to me, is greater than all; no one can snatch them out of my Father's hand. I and the Father are one."
>
> Again his Jewish opponents picked up stones to stone him, but Jesus said to them, "I have shown you many good works from the Father. For which of these do you stone me?"
>
> "We are not stoning you for any good work," they replied, "but for blasphemy, because you, a mere man, claim to be God." (John 10:24–33)

Everyone in the temple listening to this escalating discussion understood what Jesus was saying and who He claimed to be.

Another account is found in Mark 1:21–28. Jesus was teaching in the synagogue when a man in the synagogue, possessed by a demon, cried out, "What do you want with us, Jesus of Nazareth? Have you come to destroy us? I know who you are—the Holy One of God!" Jesus commanded the demon to be quiet and leave the man. The demon obeyed, and all the people who witnessed this event were amazed at Jesus' authority over demons. His power demanded obedience from demons. Even the demon knew who Jesus was.

Extrabiblical Sources Confirm Jesus' Identity

About forty years after Jesus' crucifixion, Gaius Plinius Caecilius Secundus, more commonly known as Pliny the Younger, was born. This future Roman senator and author is one of the few people from the first century who is well known because of his prolific writing. Throughout Rome's turbulent years, Pliny maintained roles that kept him closely connected to government. One of the documents he composed for the emperor included investigations and accounts of the arrested followers of "the Way" called "Christians." He explained how they were questioned, given the opportunity to recant, and if they did not recant, they were put to death. In his opinion, their beliefs were silly because they did the "strangest things"—they met at dawn, ate common food together, and worshiped a dead person they believed was God. They treated each other with outstanding love and would not worship idols. Pliny's account confirms the identity of Jesus and His followers. (For more in-depth information from Pliny and other extrabiblical sources, see the Selected Bibliography.)

The Fulfillment of Old Testament Prophecies Confirms Jesus' Identity

The Old Testament is full of prophecies about Jesus. A few of Isaiah's predictions include that Jesus will be born of a virgin,[2] will perform miracles,[3] and will be smitten and called "the Lord."[4] In the book of Micah, Jesus is prophesied to be born in the town of Bethlehem.[5] The Psalms predict that the Messiah will be the Son of God[6] and a descendent of David;[7] will be crucified, will rise from the dead, and will ascend into heaven.[8] These are just a few of the over seven hundred prophecies about Jesus.

Let's pause for a moment and catch our breath. I have covered a lot of information in these first four reasons. Much of this may be new to some of you. I've made some very broad statements in the last paragraph about fulfilled prophecies that we will unpack very specifically later in the book.

What I want you to get your mind around at this point is something very simple but profound:

- Jesus was a real person who actually lived on this planet. It is undeniable and factual. He is not a myth or a legend, but a real person who we can historically verify, not only from the Bible, but also from historians and from actual facts that we can know for certain. That may not sound like a big deal to some of you that have been followers of Christ for many years, but for some of us, the whole idea of Jesus was thrown into the "religious barrel" of fantasy thinking or mythology that we thought was made up by men.

- Jesus' actual life and lifestyle of love and kindness is validated and unquestioned by friend and foe alike.

> Jesus is not a myth or a legend, but a real person who we can historically verify.

Conclusion

As we close out this first leg of our journey together, we can know for certain that a real man named Jesus lived, that He had impeccable character and extraordinary teachings, that His miraculous powers were validated by eyewitnesses, and that He made outrageous claims about who He was and why He came.

The evidence in the first century was so strong that His enemies and detractors aimed their attacks not at His life, His teaching, or the legitimacy of His miracles, but instead, they sought to prove He was merely a great man who was a great teacher with unexplainable, great powers. That is far less than His outrageous claims that He was in fact God and the Savior of the world.

Their strategy was basic—simply prove that He didn't really die. If He didn't die, then He didn't rise from the dead. If He didn't rise from the dead, He may be a great man, a great teacher, and even have great power, but He certainly is not God or the King of Kings and Lord of Lords who has come to bring a new way of living and offer eternal life to all who believe.

In the next chapter we will answer the critic's challenge that "He really didn't die."

2

Did Jesus Really Die?

Sometimes one simple question can uncomplicate a very messy situation. I remember when my sons were in the fourth grade and they were not allowed to go into one of our neighbors' houses because their parents weren't home. There was no supervision. The use of alcohol by their teenage boys and the viewing of movies that were very inappropriate for our children made the house off-limits.

As I drove home one afternoon, I saw my twin boys exiting the house. We had a talk at dinner and I gave them a stern warning. I trusted them fully, and their explanation of just stepping inside to get their basketball seemed logical enough to me. The following week the same thing happened again, and I will never forget the conversation that we had. "Dad, you see, the thing is, we were only doing it because . . ." I listened to at least ten specific excuses and reasons why their disobedience was excusable. Every question I asked was answered by yet another list of reasons or excuses or blaming of someone else. Finally, I stopped them. I put up my hand and I said, "I have only one question for you—did you go in the house or not?" As they began another list of excuses, I stopped them yet again and asked, "Did you go in the house . . . yes or no?" The answer was an affirmative yes. "Did I tell you not to go into the house?" The answer was again an affirmative yes.

> If Jesus didn't die, He didn't rise. If He didn't rise, He's not God—He's a liar and a fake.

My point is quite simply that sometimes asking a very direct yes or no question can clear the air of all the issues, theories, conjectures, and opinions. I think this is the case when it comes to Jesus and the resurrection. Did He or didn't He die? We can talk about one million other things, but this is central. If He didn't die, He didn't rise. If He didn't rise, He's not God—He's a liar and a fake.

As we pick up our journey together, we will cover reasons 5, 6, and 7 about why I believe in the resurrection.

Reason #5: The Death of Jesus Is Undisputed

The fifth reason that I believe in the resurrection of the historical Jesus is that the evidence is overwhelming that He actually died, despite early attempts by His detractors to say that He did not. It's called "the swoon theory." He was only unconscious and appeared to be dead. The swoon theory assumes that Jesus lowered His heart rate and appeared to be dead, or that He used an ancient herb to appear unconscious. They say that Christianity is a hoax because Jesus never really died, and if He didn't die, He could not be raised from the dead.

At the time, both friend and foe were convinced that He was dead. Eyewitnesses watched Him die. The Romans were crucifixion experts, and those who buried Jesus knew first-hand that He was dead. Jesus even told His disciples that He would die but be raised from the dead three days later:

> The Son of Man must suffer many things and be rejected by the elders, the chief priests and the teachers of the law, and he must be killed and on the third day be raised to life. (Luke 9:22)

Jesus' death is undisputed. It really happened. Let's take a look at the evidence.

At Jesus' crucifixion, both those who loved Jesus, as well as those who mocked Him and cried out for His death, were present. Jesus' mother, Mary, Mary Magdalene, John, and other followers of Jesus were there. The chief priest and scribes were there, and they mocked Him by saying, "He saved others, but he can't save himself!" (Matt. 27:42).

The Roman soldiers were there and they testified to Jesus' death. They did not break Jesus' legs, which was customary in crucifixion, because He had already died. Later, they pierced His side to further confirm His death. A Roman centurion even assured Pilate of Jesus' death.

> Pilate was surprised to hear that he was already dead. Summoning the centurion, he asked him if Jesus had already died. When he learned from the centurion that it was so, he gave the body to Joseph. (Mark 15:44–45)

The Romans were professional executioners. Crucifixion was the preferred method for capital punishment, and it caused excruciating suffering and certain death from suffocation. It was a horrifying, humiliating, and public way to die. In crucifixion, the person being put to death was stripped of clothing and, in a public place, securely hung on a T-shaped beam using rope or nails. The victim was completely powerless to defend himself.

The way a victim hung required them to push up with their legs and pull up with outstretched arms to catch a breath. After each breath, the person would then sink back down to start the entire process all over again. When they could no longer push or pull up to take a breath, suffocation and death quickly followed. Depending on the situation, this process could take up to several days. If a crucifixion was taking too long, the executioners would break the victim's legs to speed up the process. This form of death is one of the most agonizingly painful ways invented by man.

As I said before, the Romans were professional executioners. They were skilled because of how many people they had executed through crucifixion. So when the Romans came to check on Jesus to see how He was progressing, they saw He was dead and did not break His legs (John 19:33, 36). This is another fulfillment of Old Testament prophecies (Num. 9:12; Ps. 34:20; Exod. 12:46).

Let's think about all that Jesus went through. Before being crucified, He endured intense flogging. He was flogged with thirty-nine lashes. It was thirty-nine, because most people could not live past thirty-nine. If you've seen the movie *The Passion of the Christ*, it accurately portrays this event in

Jesus' life. The person being flogged would have their arms wrapped and tied around a pole in order to stretch out the skin on the back. A stick or a rod with rawhide strips containing metal balls and pieces of bone attached to the end was used to whip the victim. The goal was to snap it in such a way that the metal balls would hit, causing contusions and internal bleeding. It would then wrap around the victim so when it was pulled away, the pieces of bone would rip the flesh.

> The medical evidence is clear that Jesus was truly dead.

All of this was done to Jesus before a crown of thorns was forced on His head and He was taken to be crucified (Matt. 27:26). He was within an inch of His life before He ever went to the cross. He didn't even have the strength to carry the beam He was to be crucified on (Matt. 27:32). The intensity of the flogging and the crucifixion was powerful and deadly.

There is also medical evidence to support the death of Jesus. To ensure and confirm Jesus' death, a Roman soldier pierced His side with a spear, "bringing a sudden flow of blood and water" (John 19:34). The pericardial sac that surrounds your heart is filled with clear fluid. When the spear pierced Jesus' side, it went through His heart, releasing the fluid from the pericardial sac, mixing with His blood. Medically, when the blood and fluid flow from a heart wound, death has occurred. The medical evidence is clear that Jesus was truly dead.

Jesus' burial preparation provides additional evidence of His death. After Jesus had died, Joseph of Arimathea and Nicodemus, two of the religious leaders who didn't agree with Jesus' crucifixion, asked for His body. Pilate gave Joseph permission and Joseph took Jesus' body to be buried in his own tomb (John 19:38–40). We learn from Scripture that they prepared Jesus' body with myrrh and spices. According to burial practices in that time, they would take strips of linen with myrrh and spices and would wrap it around the body. In total they would use about seventy pounds of linen, myrrh, and spices. The entire body was wrapped, including a facecloth. History and medical science provides undisputed evidence that Jesus was fully dead.

Reason #6: The Burial of Jesus Was Public and Secured

The sixth reason I believe in the resurrection of the historical Jesus is that the burial of Jesus was public and secured. Some of the detractors would say, "Well, you know what? He really died, but they went to the wrong tomb or the disciples stole the body." Because the Pharisees were concerned that the disciples would steal the body and tell everyone that Jesus rose from the dead, they went to Pilate and asked for help (Matt. 27:62–66). Pilate responded by placing a Roman guard to watch and protect Jesus' tomb.

We know from Scripture that the tomb was empty, and all that remained was the burial linen neatly folded. The chief priests decided the best course of action was to bribe the soldiers to say that the disciples stole the body while they slept (Matt. 28:11–13). How would sleeping guards be able to see what was happening?

The burial of Jesus was public knowledge and it was very secure. Only Jesus, the Son of God, could have the awesome power to overcome death.

The security of the tomb is undisputed. The tomb Jesus was buried in belonged to Joseph of Arimathea, a wealthy man in high standing in the community. The security of a wealthy man's tomb was important and this tomb was carved out of solid rock. It was the Rolls-Royce of tombs. I had the opportunity to go to Israel a number of years ago and toured the tombs. Despite all the commercialism and speculation around Jesus' tomb, the quality of the tombs of the rich was very evident. Jesus' body was in a secure and well-known location.

The Roman guards kept the tomb secure. The discipline, weaponry, and brutal force of the Roman army made it one of the strongest fighting forces the world had ever seen. I would not want to go up against one of those well-trained warriors. Capital punishment for falling asleep or failing at their duty kept the guards' attention flawless. They would not willingly have allowed anyone to steal Jesus' body.

The Roman seal was an insignia representing the power and authority of Rome. It was used to guarantee that there would be no tampering with official business. The breaking of a seal brought the full wrath of Rome and was punishable by immediate death. Roman seals were effective and people left them alone. The tomb was secure, and the seal was unbroken from the outside.

Jesus was securely buried in a tomb carved out of solid rock and the stone that sealed the entrance was extremely heavy. The large stone followed a ridge and would drop into place at the entrance of the tomb. It took four or five men to drop the stone into place and it would take a great many more to lift and roll the stone away. There was no way that twenty men could sneak by or overpower the Roman soldiers, then lift the stone away and take Jesus' body.

Reason #7: The Evidence Is Convincing and Reasonable

The seventh and final reason I believe in Jesus' resurrection is that the evidence for it is convincing and reasonable. There is intellectual, historical, verifiable evidence. I will not throw my brains in the trash to believe, and you do not have to either.

In a courtroom, for a case to win, it must be legally convincing beyond reasonable doubt. Today when people are tried, eyewitnesses are called to testify, experts give testimony, circumstances are examined, evidence is collected, history is reviewed, and motives are taken into account. No one on the jury was a firsthand witness to verify every specific detail of the case; however, a decision must be made. In order for a final decision to be made, the evidence must prove to be beyond a reasonable doubt.

What is the evidence in the case for the resurrection? Is the evidence convincing and reasonable? I have carefully researched the resurrection and asked myself what is the preponderance of the evidence? I want to share with you the specific evidences that led me to believe in the resurrection of Jesus Christ.

Exhibit A: It was predicted by the Old Testament prophets.

The Old Testament prophets predicted the life, death, and resurrection of Jesus hundreds of years before it happened. After examining the many prophecies from the Old Testament, I was convinced beyond reasonable doubt. I encourage you to examine them for yourself.

Isaiah 53:5

> But he was pierced for our transgressions,
>   he was crushed for our iniquities;
> the punishment that brought us peace was on him,
>   and by his wounds we are healed.

Isaiah 53:7

> He was oppressed and afflicted,
>   yet he did not open his mouth;
> he was led like a lamb to the slaughter,
>   and as a sheep before its shearers is silent,
> so he did not open his mouth.

Isaiah 53:9

> He was assigned a grave with the wicked,
>   and with the rich in his death,
> though he had done no violence,
>   nor was any deceit in his mouth.

Psalm 22:16–18

> Dogs surround me,
>   a pack of villains encircles me;
>   they pierce my hands and my feet.
> All my bones are on display;
>   people stare and gloat over me.
> They divide my clothes among them
>   and cast lots for my garment.

Exhibit B: Jesus predicted it openly numerous times.

In the second half of Jesus' ministry on earth, His death and resurrection three days later was a major theme of His teaching to His followers.

John 2:18–22

The Jews then responded to him, "What sign can you show us to prove your authority to do all this?" Jesus answered them, "Destroy this temple, and I will raise it again in three days."

They replied, "It has taken forty-six years to build this temple, and you are going to raise it in three days?" But the temple he had spoken of was his body. After he was raised from the dead, his disciples recalled what he had said. Then they believed the scripture and the words that Jesus had spoken.

John 10:17–18

The reason my Father loves me is that I lay down my life—only to take it up again. No one takes it from me, but I lay it down of my own accord. I have authority to lay it down and authority to take it up again. This command I received from my Father.

Matthew 16:21

From that time on Jesus began to explain to his disciples that he must go to Jerusalem and suffer many things at the hands of the elders, the chief priests and the teachers of the law, and that he must be killed and on the third day be raised to life.

Matthew 27:62–64

The next day, the one after Preparation Day, the chief priests and the Pharisees went to Pilate. "Sir," they said, "we remember that while he was still alive that deceiver said, 'After three days I will rise again.' So give the order for the tomb to be made secure until the third day. Otherwise, his disciples may come and steal the body and tell the people that he has been raised from the dead. This last deception will be worse than the first."

Exhibit C: The testimony of women.

A strong evidence for the truth of Jesus' resurrection is the presence of the women at the tomb and inclusion of their testimony by the Gospel writers. At that time, the testimony of women in civil and criminal hearings was considered worthless. And yet it is to women that God gives the experience of being the first eyewitnesses of Jesus' empty tomb and the joyful responsibility of sharing the good news with others. If the writers were trying to validate a false claim, why would they include the testimony of women? It would make more sense to insert males into the role of first witnesses.

Exhibit D: He appeared twelve different times to over five hundred witnesses.

For forty days after His resurrection, Jesus walked around in His resurrected body and appeared to over five hundred people in multiple locations. They saw Him, they talked with Him, they ate with Him, and they heard Him teach about the kingdom of God.

He appeared to

- The women (Luke 24:1–12)
- The two disciples on the Emmaus Road (Luke 24:18–32)
- The disciples minus Thomas (John 20:19–24)
- Peter and the disciples (John 21:1–14)
- More than five hundred of the brothers and sisters at the same time (1 Cor. 15:6)

Exhibit E: The transformation of the disciples.

The disciples went from a group of fearful, selfish, ordinary men to a powerful group of spiritual leaders who ultimately changed the world. After Jesus' earthly ministry was complete and He ascended to heaven, the disciples led and grew the early church. Their faith was rooted in the day-to-day experiences they had with Jesus.

Exhibit F: He appeared in multiple locations and times for over forty days.

One argument claims that the resurrection could not be true because the appearance of Jesus was only a hallucination brought on by an extreme desire to see Him again. Research done by psychologists has verified that hallucinations can happen, but they rarely, if ever, occur in groups. It is impossible for a group of people to have the same hallucination in multiple locations. Jesus' appearance was not a hallucination.

Exhibit G: The explosion of the early church.

The church grew exponentially in the first twenty-five years following the resurrection. What was so dynamic about this time was that people could verify their faith through conversations with eyewitnesses of the resurrection.

Exhibit H: It is not logical—in fact, it is inconceivable—for the disciples to willingly and knowingly "die for a lie."

Tragically, in our day we know people are willing to die for something they believe in. No one, however, would willingly die for what they know is a lie. It's inconceivable for the disciples to say: "You know what? Let's steal Jesus' body because He said He would come back, and although He didn't, let's keep this movement going. Everyone is trying to kill us for teaching that He is still alive, so let's keep it up and die." It does not make intellectual sense for the disciples to die for a lie.

Exhibit I: The conversion of Saul of Tarsus.

Will Durant is a twentieth-century secular American expert on the history of civilization. He has written volumes on the subject and this is what he says about the conversion of Saul of Tarsus in his book *Caesar and Christ*: "No one can say what natural processes underlay this pivotal experience."[1] I would say that is because natural processes are totally inadequate to answer to the cause for the change that took place in this man.

> No one would willingly die for what they know is a lie.

Saul was a Roman citizen, born into an elite family and given the best education. He was trained under Gamaliel and studied at the Ivy League school of his day. He was a brilliant man and a fervent persecutor of Christians. He genuinely believed he was doing the right thing by threatening, imprisoning, and killing followers of Christ. He experienced a complete 180 in his life.

Imagine in our day, this would be like the leader of North Korea coming on television and saying, "I repudiate everything I have said and everything I believe. I am now a human rights activist. I care for the downtrodden, I want to help people, and I'm freeing everyone in North Korea. I'm going to go all around the world and help anybody who is trapped in marginalized dictatorships to find life, help, and peace. This is my new purpose in life."

How would we respond? First of all, most of us would think, "Yeah, right." The followers of Jesus had the same response to Paul's conversion. They thought there was no way this was possible, and the early apostles didn't even want to associate with him. They thought it had to be a trick. His life was radically changed. He went from "breathing out murderous threats against the Lord's disciples" (Acts 9:1) to "preach[ing] in the synagogue that Jesus is the Son of God" (Acts 9:20). Paul went on to write thirteen books in the New Testament and suffered more for his commitment to Christ than any other apostle.

Exhibit J: The transformation of the Roman Empire and the world.

The Roman Empire in the first century was polytheistic, powerful, and evil. Jesus and the twelve disciples ministered for three years and launched a movement that changed the world.

The early group of followers grew to 120 people, definitely not a megachurch, when Jesus ascended into heaven, leaving His followers with a mission to reach the world with His message. They changed their communities and the world by the way they lived their lives. They lived as though Jesus was alive through them. They purposed to act, speak, and live the way Jesus lived. Lepers were touched, disenfranchised were loved, and people were united in the mission to care for others. The cultural labels that once divided people were deliberately set aside for the opportunity to love one another. Miracles occurred and lives were changed.

The followers of Jesus continued to grow exponentially, even as persecution intensified. They walked arm in arm into stadiums before thousands of people and sang hymns of thanks to God as wild beasts were let loose to tear them apart. Nero preferred to use Christians as lighting in his gardens. He had Christians impaled on poles and set on fire. People still chose to follow Jesus.

In today's world, people are disowned by their family, thrown in prison, tortured, shot, beheaded, and even crucified for following Jesus. Yet His people still choose to believe the resurrected Jesus is God's Son and follow Him.

Sociologist Rodney Stark, in two seminal books—one called *The Rise of Christianity* and the other called *The Triumph of Christianity*—observes that there were three major plagues in the first eighty to one hundred years of the church, and tens of thousands or hundreds of thousands and even entire cities were wiped out. The only people who stayed in the cities to nurse people back to health were Christians, and they were viewed as martyrs. Massive numbers of Christians died, giving their lives to save people during these plagues. What possesses a group of people to give their lives for the lives of others? It is the power of the resurrected Christ living inside of them. As a result, by AD 313, during the reign of Constantine, it is estimated that of the 60 million people in the Roman Empire, 33 million were followers of Christ.

Exhibit K: The best legal minds state the evidence is conclusive.

Through my studies on the resurrection, I came across the work of Simon Greenleaf, a professor and major contributor to the development of Harvard Law School. In his book *The Testimony of the Evangelists: Examined by the Rules of Evidence Administered in Courts of Justice*, Greenleaf applied the principles of "rule of law" and "examination of evidence" to the resurrection and New Testament documents. After a thorough evaluation of the evidence Greenleaf says,

All that Christianity asks of men on this subject is, that they would be consistent with themselves; that they would treat its evidences as they treat the evidence of other things; and that they would try and judge its actors and witnesses, as they deal with their fellow men, when testifying to human affairs and actions in human tribunals. Let the witnesses be compared with themselves, with each other, and with the surrounding facts and circumstances; and let their testimony be sifted, as if it were given in a court of justice, on the side of the adverse party, the witness being subjected to rigorous cross-examination. The result, it is confidently believed will be an undoubting conviction of their integrity, ability, and truth.[2]

Over the years, a number of people have attempted to write books to disprove the resurrection; but as they evaluated the evidence, their books took a drastic turn in a new direction. What were intended to be books that revealed the myth of Jesus Christ's resurrection became books that supported it.

Frank Morrison, a lawyer, was one of these people. He wanted to write a book that refuted Christianity and Jesus' resurrection, but the more he weighed the evidence, the more he was compelled to believe in Jesus. Through the process of his investigation, he became a follower of Jesus and his book disproving the resurrection became, as Morrison says, "the book that refused to be written." Instead he wrote *Who Moved the Stone?*, and it has been an inspiration to many people in their search for truth.

C. S. Lewis was an agnostic professor at both Oxford and Cambridge. Conversations with his friends challenged him to evaluate the evidence for Christianity and his conclusions led him to faith in Jesus Christ and to write *Mere Christianity*.

Sir Lionel Luckhoo is a defense attorney listed in the 1990 *Guinness Book of World Records* as the "world's most suc-cessful lawyer" for pleading the cases and winning 245 successive acquittals for his clients. His testimony in *Leading Lawyers Look at the Resurrection* declares, "I have spent more than forty-two years as a defense trial lawyer appearing in many parts of the world . . . I say unequivocally the evidence for the resurrection of Jesus Christ is so over-whelming that it compels acceptance by proof which leaves absolutely no doubt."[3]

> What were intended to be books that revealed the myth of Jesus Christ's resurrection became books that supported it.

When you look at all this evidence, are you able to answer beyond a reasonable doubt that Jesus is in fact who He claimed to be?

Exhibit L: He changed my life.

The final evidence for me is a very personal one. It is what the resurrected Jesus has done in my life.

You know why I believe in Jesus? It includes the word *Punkie*. Why any parent would name their daughter that, I don't know, but my parents did. Punkie is my sister.

While I was in high school, my dad's alcoholism was getting worse. My older sister responded by rebelling and going off to college, and my sister Punkie wrestled with an eating disorder. Being "the rescuer" in an alcoholic family, I became a workaholic and tried to figure out how to make life work for our family. I was the youngest child and it was a heavy

49

burden for me to carry. Punkie loved me like no one had ever loved me in my life. She was the kindest, most unselfish, most considerate, most caring person I had ever known.

Unbeknownst to me, a couple of years earlier in high school, Punkie became a Christian, a genuine follower of Jesus. I saw a change in her life, but I couldn't explain it. She didn't preach at or nag me, she just loved me through her words and actions. I would walk into the house with my basketball buddies, and she would say, "Would you guys like a sandwich?" Or I would have a test and she would help me study for it. She was that person who was always there for me.

When I was tempted to do stuff that I knew was really bad, I would ask myself, what would Punkie think? I didn't want to disappoint her. Have you ever had someone love you like that?

Someday, someway, I thought, I wanted to be like her. Her life was amazing. But I didn't know why. She introduced me to some people who eventually piqued my interest in taking a fresh look at God, the Bible, and Christianity. To say my life changed and is changing is an understatement. In fact, about ten years ago, a fellow high school basketball player who had become a Christian saw my name on the internet and wondered if it could be the same Chip Ingram. We were both unbelievers in high school and had attitudes and lifestyles to prove it. He called and said he couldn't believe I was a pastor leading a Christian organization; he only knew the "Old Chip."

I want to share with you one final evidence of God's loving work in my life, and that's my youngest granddaughter. She is one year old, and the other day she wanted to color eggs.

I don't really like to color eggs, but I couldn't resist. She just learned how to kiss, and her mommy said, "Kiss Papa." She leaned over, looked me in the eyes, and gave me a kiss. She's our tenth grandchild from our four adult children who have all grown up to love Christ, marry fellow believers, and produce this amazing extended family. Some of you might be able to grasp what a miracle that is since my wife and I both came from alcoholic families.

I love that little girl. And the trajectory of her life is off-the-charts different than my family of origin because I met the resurrected Christ. He radically changed my life, my values, my priorities, and my family. That's how it works . . . one life at a time.

Conclusion

Wow, what a journey this has been. I have shared why I believe in the resurrection, and there are three very specific implications that you and I need to ponder.

1. *The first implication is, what does it mean to you?* I would say the evidence validates Jesus' claim, "I am the way and the truth and the life. No one comes to the Father except through Me" (John 14:6). His claim is unique, extreme, and narrow, and it's proven by the resurrection. It is either true or false. There is no middle ground.

   > Jesus radically changed my life, my values, my priorities, and my family.

2. *The second implication is that the resurrection gives absolute hope for the future.* Jesus said,

"Because I live, you will live." Can I tell you something? I am not afraid of terrorists. I am not afraid to travel. I am not afraid of global economic crisis. I am not afraid of the stock market crashing. Throughout history the church and God's people have gone through repeated ups and downs, but I put my trust in God.

God is in absolute control. No matter what I go through, He is with me. When I die, I will go immediately into the presence of Jesus Christ, not because I am a good person, not because I am a pastor, and not because I have done something special. It's because I have believed and trusted in Jesus' death on the cross as the full payment for sins and received His forgiveness of my sin. I have repented of my sin and my self-will and asked Him to come into my life. He has forgiven me and He lives in me. Because Jesus lives, I live, and He offers that to whoever believes.

3. *The third implication is eternal life.* It's not something in the future. It's something that starts now. Let's take a look at a very popular verse that you may have heard or even seen in the NFL end zone . . .

> For God so loved the world that he gave his one and only Son, that whoever believes in him shall not perish but have eternal life. (John 3:16)

Read this verse aloud again and actually insert your name into it. "For God so loved" and say your name to yourself. I want you to know and feel that this is true. This is the greatest act of love toward you in the world.

> For God so loved [*your name*] that he gave his one and only Son that if [*your name*] believes in him, [*your

name] shall not perish but have eternal life. For God did not send his Son into the world to condemn [*your name*], but to save [*your name*] through him.

For the great majority of you who are reading this book, you know exactly what I'm talking about. You have already put your faith in Christ. You can remember the day you prayed and asked Jesus to forgive your sins and come into your life.

But the truth is, the world has changed a lot in the last several years. In addition, many of the things that you were taught to believe are being challenged even in evangelical churches. It's becoming more difficult and more unpopular to be a follower of Jesus, and often doubts crowd in when pressure increases.

It's easy to feel out of step or anti-intellectual to say that you are a follower of Jesus and believe the Bible and the resurrection. This chapter is a reminder from God that you haven't thrown your brains in the trash and that your intellectual standing is historical, logical, and well-founded.

For others, a friend has given you this book because you used to go to church, or you are spiritual and honestly seeking for the truth and wonder about Jesus and the claims of Christianity. Let me first say thank you for joining me on this journey. I remember well honestly wondering about life and God and my purpose on the earth. I wondered if what is written about Jesus and His claims to be God and to give me eternal life could be true.

So let me encourage you to look at yourself as the member of a jury examining all that you've read in these first two chapters and to honestly weigh the evidence. Think it over, talk about it with a friend, make a list of the things that make sense and the things that you still question. It is a journey, but there is a God who loves you and wants to reveal Himself to you.

> Look at yourself as the member of a jury examining all that you've read and honestly weigh the evidence.

Finally, let me encourage you to pray a little prayer that I prayed as I was on my journey. No one gave it to me, but it just seemed to make a lot of sense, and it's one I know that God will answer . . .

> *"God, if you exist, please reveal Yourself to me in a way that I can really understand. I want You to know that if You do it in a way that I can understand, I will do whatever You want me to do. Amen."*

God promises that if you seek Him with all your heart, you will find Him.

Finally, the resurrection is certainly the centerpiece of Christianity and a relationship with God through Jesus Christ. But if you're like me, I had a lot of questions that went beyond the resurrection. And the biggest one by far was, "Can I really trust the Bible?" So much of what I've shared and what Jesus taught is in the Bible, but what if it is not true? What if the Bible has been changed and corrupted over the years? How could I really know that the Bible is not just an old book instead of the very Word of God?

Well, grab a cup of coffee and let's look at these questions together in the next two chapters.

3

Why I Believe in the Bible

Jesus answered, "It is written: 'Man shall not live on bread alone, but on every word that comes from the mouth of God.'"

Matthew 4:4

The Bible is the bestselling book of all time with over five billion copies sold and distributed. Eighty-eight percent of American homes own a Bible and over 180 million users worldwide have downloaded a Bible app for their mobile device. Despite having the Bible at our fingertips, there is growing confusion about the authority of the Bible and how it impacts our lives.

When I was growing up, my family had a large, heavy Bible that we kept on display on our coffee table. That seemed to be a common practice in many homes in those days. When we picked it up, it was usually to dust the table, not to read it. When I was twelve years old, I had a spiritual desire to actually read the Bible. I had a sense that maybe there was something important in it. Have you ever had an unexplainable spiritual urge to pray or read the Bible? Well, that's how I felt.

My parents were out of the house on an errand, and I found myself being drawn to the living room. I went over to the coffee table and opened the Bible. I had a thirty-five-second experience that went something like this: "Hitherto, unto thine own, the Hittites and the Gibeonites and the Mishishites and the Shupashites and the Michegites and the Ucheites. Hitherto thine own . . ." I quickly closed the Bible and put it back in its place on the coffee table. I walked away with the feeling that I didn't know anything about the Bible, and I had no hope of ever being able to understand it. It was a complete mystery to me.

Fast-forward to when I was eighteen years old. Basketball was a very important part of my life and I played every opportunity I could get. A coach paid my way to attend a basketball camp run by the Fellowship of Christian Athletes. When I got there, they gave me a New Testament. It was easy to read and understand, but this time I didn't want to read it. I didn't want to be indoctrinated with their Jesus stuff. All I wanted to do was play basketball.

After playing basketball with the guys at camp and watching how they authentically loved Jesus, I came to the conclusion that I owed it to myself to give the Bible another shot. I should at least read the New Testament with an open mind to see if what it said could be remotely true.

Fast-forward yet again. I had been a Christian for about five years, had traveled overseas, and had watched God at work in those places. While I was in graduate school at West Virginia University, I walked to class with a Bible in my hand, and one of my PhD classmates asked me, "So, is that a Bible?" And I said, "Yeah!" And he said, "Well, you don't believe that, do you?" I replied, "Well, actually, I do." He started laughing and he asked, "Why?" I mumbled something about how it really changed my life. He asked me a number of other penetrating questions, and I realized that I did not have good answers for him or for myself.

Here are five questions that really caused me to think about what I believed and challenged me to find answers.

- Is the Bible the word of men or the very words of God?
- Is the Bible full of myths, legends, and fairy tales, or is it historically reliable?
- Is ALL of the Bible true and trustworthy or only portions of it?
- Can a Bible that has been translated so many times over so many years really be accurate?
- What makes the Bible so different from all the other religious writings and their claims to truth?

> I should at least read the New Testament with an open mind to see if what it said could be remotely true.

The underlying question . . . *Is it intellectually feasible to believe that the Bible could be God's Word?*

In this chapter and the next, I want to share with you why I believe the Bible is God's Word. As we journey through the chapter together, we will revisit the questions I was asked, and it's my hope that you will ask yourself, what do I really believe?

Reason #1: Archaeology

Archaeological evidence supports the fact that the Bible is full of real places, people, and events throughout time. The Bible is the Word of God and not a collection of myths, fairy tales, or oral stories handed down to teach good moral lessons.

Through the years, the historicity and authorship of the Bible have been challenged at multiple levels. At the turn of the last century, popular belief claimed that the Bible was just a collection of good thoughts from God, but not the actual Word of God. Opponents pointed to the lack of archaeological evidence as proof that the Bible could neither be the Word of God nor a trusted historical document.

One of the major arguments against its historical accuracy was a lack of such evidence for a group of people called the Hittites. Liberal scholars accused the Bible of being unreliable because it contained accounts of a Hittite civilization of which there was no record. Over the last 150 years, archaeologists have uncovered Hittite ruins, artifacts, and ten thousand clay tablets from the royal archives. Now there is no doubt of the Hittite's flourishing civilization.[1]

Another evidence for the historicity of the Bible is the Merneptah Stele. This inscription by an ancient Egyptian king, dating back to 1207 BC, was discovered in 1896 and is the earliest connection between archaeology and the Bible. It verifies that a people called "Israel" really did exist and lived in the land of Canaan following the Exodus.[2]

In 1993, an Israeli archaeologist discovered the first mention of King David outside of the Bible. The Tel Dan inscription, a writing on a ninth-century stone tablet, commemorates an

Aramean king's defeat of his southern enemies, the "king of Israel" and the "king of the House of David." It is clear from this inscription that King David was a real person, and even though this event took place centuries after David's lifetime, his fame was still known by foreign enemies.[3]

In the early 1900s, Sir William Ramsay, a famous archaeologist and historian, was highly skeptical of the historical reliability of the New Testament. After reading the book of Acts, he set out to prove that it was an unreliable historical document and full of errors. He spent fourteen years in Israel looking for evidence to disprove Luke's account. After examining the evidence, he emerged from his study to announce that "Luke is a historian of the first rank; not merely are his statements of fact trustworthy . . . this author should be placed along with the very greatest historians."[4]

> "Luke is a historian of the first rank; not merely are his statements of fact trustworthy . . . this author should be placed along with the very greatest historians."
>
> —Sir William Ramsay

Dr. Nelson Glueck, an American rabbi and archaeologist, discovered over 1,500 ancient sites in Israel. He said,

> It may be stated categorically that no archaeological discovery has ever controverted a Biblical reference. Scores of archaeological findings have been made which confirm in clear outline or in exact detail historical statements in the Bible. And, by the same token, proper evaluation of biblical descriptions has often led to amazing discoveries. They form tesserae in the vast mosaic of the Bible's almost incredibly correct historical memory.[5]

My faith is not based on a story told by someone who claimed to have had an experience with God, then wrote a book and said I should follow it. The Bible is a historically reliable, accurate document.

Reason #2: Revelation

I believe in the Bible because of revelation. The Bible claims to infallibly reveal the very words and mind of God. Now, step back for just a second to ponder this incredible claim.

I am an early riser and enjoy the wee hours of the morning before the sun comes up. I purposefully turn off the lights in the house, take my cup of coffee, and walk out into my backyard to look up at all the stars. The immense sky full of stars is amazing. Whenever I gaze at the stars, I always think to myself, for thousands of years people have looked up into the sky and have seen the same stars I am looking at right now. Scripture tells me that God spoke the world into existence (Gen. 1) and the One who spoke those words wants to be known. Psalm 19:1 says, "The heavens declare the glory of God; the skies proclaim the work of his hands." God's power and majesty are revealed through creation.

About halfway through my cup of coffee, it always hits me that God did not stop there, but He wants me to know Him personally. Then I go into my study, I open up my Bible and read the words of God. I am literally in awe that the God who spoke galaxies into existence would actually speak to me through the Bible.

There are many religious books that offer wisdom, but the Bible claims far more than that. The unique claim of the Bible is that it is the very Word of God. Second Timothy 3:16 says that all Scripture is inspired by God—literally, God-breathed—and is profitable for teaching, for reproof, for correcting, and for training in righteousness. The next verse goes on to say that the man or woman of God might be equipped for every good work. In other words, the Bible is not simply a written proposition or even truth for life; it is far more.

> The unique claim of the Bible is that it is the very Word of God.

The Bible claims itself to be an active, powerful force in our lives. "For the word of God is living and active and sharper than any two-edged sword piercing to the division of soul and spirit, joints and of marrow, and discerning the thoughts and intentions of the heart" (Heb. 4:12 NASB).

These passages make the astounding claim that God's Word, the Bible, is actually inspired by Him, and that He can be personally known and experienced through the Scriptures.

All Scripture—Both the Old and the New Testaments

I'm often asked when it comes to the inspiration of God's Word, does that apply to both the Old and the New Testaments? The answer is yes, and it's supported by the two great apostles in the New Testament—the apostle Paul and the apostle Peter. The apostle Paul wrote in 1 Timothy 5:18: "For Scripture says, 'Do not muzzle an ox while it is treading out the grain,' and 'The worker deserves his wages.'" Notice that he refers to this passage out of the book of Proverbs in the Old Testament as Scripture.

We also see the New Testament referred to as Scripture by the apostle Peter as he equates the authority of the letters of Paul with the Old Testament scriptures. Peter says in 2 Peter 3:16 concerning Paul, "He [Paul] writes the same way in all his letters, speaking in them of these matters. His letters contain some things that are hard to understand, which ignorant and unstable people distort, as they do the other Scriptures to their own destruction." Jesus and His apostles viewed the Old Testament as Scripture, God-breathed words for us in printed form. As the Spirit of God applies the written Word in our lives, it becomes the living Word.

> The truths of Jesus and Scripture always bring us to a crossroad.

The Bible claims to be the authoritative, inspired words of God. Over three thousand times we read in the Bible, "thus says the Lord." It is an exclusive claim. The truths of Jesus and Scripture always bring us to a crossroad where we must intellectually decide what we believe. I believe that the Bible's claim to be revelation is a vital cornerstone in building an intellectually feasible case that the Bible really is the Word of God.

Reason #3: Origin

The origin of the Bible is another reason why I believe the Bible is God's Word. The Bible's unity, structure, and subject matter argue for a supernatural authorship. Have you ever imagined how all of this could possibly come together? It would have to be miraculous.

It had to be the strangest publishing project of all time. No editor or publishing house was responsible for forty independent authors representing twenty occupations, living in ten countries during a fifteen-hundred-year span, working in three languages with a cast of two thousand nine hundred and thirty characters in fifteen hundred and fifty places. And together they produced sixty-six books containing eleven hundred and eighty-nine chapters. And from every conceivable form: prose, poetry, romance, mystery, biography, science, and history. What was the final product? The Bible. One evidence that the Bible is a supernatural book is the unity that it displays, despite such wide differences among authors, cultures, and forms of expression.[6]

For over fifteen hundred years, the central theme from Genesis all the way to Revelation was the Messiah. The Old Testament pointed to the Messiah's coming, the New Testament revealed His presence and His name, Jesus Christ. The Gospels told His story and the book of Acts showed us how the apostles followed through with Jesus' Great Commission. The letters told us how the early church, a revolutionary movement, took the love of God to the ends of the earth. Jesus' return and the fulfillment of His promises climax in the book of Revelation. The Bible is a one-of-a-kind book.

Let's take a minute to let that sink in and put it in perspective. Can you think back to your high school, college, or graduate school days? Do you remember group projects? A huge assignment would be handed out to your group of four or five people. Everyone would tackle a portion of the work, do research, write a paper, and collaborate together to successfully finish the project.

It is very difficult to do your research and get four other people on the same page so that the project is done well and completed on time. There is always that one person who doesn't pull their weight. Did you ever feel that it would just be easier to do the work yourself?

God did not choose to drop an impersonal book of words from heaven. Instead, He inspired authors throughout fifteen hundred years, twenty different professions, multiple cultures, thousands of miles from one another, with an amazing alignment that even prophecies made over a thousand years earlier would be fulfilled. God is an eloquent, powerful, and personal communicator. God supernaturally inspired and preserved the Bible that you hold in your hands. It is an amazing phenomenon. In fact, it is miraculous.

Reason #4: Authenticity

Another reason why I believe the Bible is the Word of God is because it contains such honest accounts. My daughter is a millennial, and over the years we have had many late-twentysomethings to early-thirtysomethings in our home. As I listened to these young professionals share about their lives and what was important to them, I repeatedly heard them use the word "authentic." Authenticity is a high value for many people, but this generation seems to have a visceral reaction to anything they sense as fake. They would rather see clearly in the light what another generation would choose to keep in the dark. The lives of the people in the Bible are genuine and not touched up to give a good impression. We see their struggles, failures, and pain, as well as their triumphs.

> The lives of the people in the Bible are genuine and not touched up to give a good impression.

Take Abraham, for example, God's friend with whom He made a covenant to bless the world. Abraham was not perfect.

He lied repeatedly out of fear to protect his life, even putting his wife at risk to do so. Not a very flattering picture of the patriarch of our faith. He was impatient at times; instead of waiting on God to provide a son, he took things into his own hands and had a child named Ishmael with his wife's maid. He made wrong choices that impacted his world, and the impact of those choices is still felt today.

David, the mighty king of Israel, the man after God's own heart, was not perfect either. He committed adultery and murder. Peter promised to always stand by Jesus and then completely betrayed Him hours later. The apostle Paul persecuted and murdered people in the name of God.

The Bible does not hide people behind a mask of human perfection. When you read the Bible, you get an accurate depiction of the human heart and human nature. In contrast, the Bible reveals the gracious and merciful heart of God. You see the very depth of His forgiveness and you see ordinary people like you and me being transformed from the inside out.

Reason #5: Jesus

Jesus believed the Old Testament to be the very words of God and predicted that the New Testament would be likewise. Pause for a moment with me and ponder the implications of that statement. It was this one point probably more than any other that convinced me of the Bible's validity in being the Word of God. Let's follow the logic together:

> The Bible does not hide people behind a mask of human perfection.

1. We have very good reasons to believe that the Bible is a historically accurate document concerning people, places, and the life and works of Jesus.
2. If the Bible is historically reliable, then there is strong evidence for believing that Jesus was who He said He was—God's Son and the Savior of the world.
3. Because Jesus is God's Son, we can have absolute confidence in what He says about the Bible being inspired by God.

Let me put it another way. I've had the privilege of serving on three different juries in my lifetime. Some involved very serious crimes, and the decision that we made had great implications for a person's life. Throughout the trials, experts in ballistics or forensic medicine would give testimony that often shed such light about the facts that our decision regarding guilt or innocence became obvious.

Jesus is the greatest expert witness on the Bible. His view of it carries extraordinary weight because He not only claimed to be the Son of God, He lived a perfect life, died, and rose again. So let's look at how he viewed the Old Testament and what He would say later alluding to the New Testament.

Jesus had much to say about God's Word, and the list below provides a great overview of what He believed about the Old Testament's authority, reliability, and accuracy:

1. It was divinely inspired— Matt. 22:31–32; 43.
2. It was without error and infallible—John 10:35; 17:17; Matt. 22:29.
3. It is the final authority—Matt. 4:4, 7, 10.

4. It is historically reliable. Jesus believed in a literal Adam and Eve—Matt. 19:4–5; Noah and the ark and a world-wide flood—Matt. 24:37; the literal life and faith of Abraham—John 8:56; the destruction of Sodom—Luke 17:29, 32; the law as given by Moses—John 7:19; Matt. 19:18; manna given in the wilderness—John 6:31–51; as well as the historical life of David, the queen of Sheba, Solomon, Elijah, and even the story of Jonah and the great fish.

5. The Scripture was sufficient for life and faith—Luke 16:31.[7]

Jesus believed the extent of the Old Testament authority included

1. The very words of Scripture—Luke 24:44.
2. The specific tenses of verbs—Matt. 22:32.
3. The smallest portion of the letters in words were inspired—Matt. 5:17–18.[8]

The list above of Jesus' view of the Bible is pretty overwhelming, but I've heard people say that we're not expected to take those statements literally; that it's not like every word is God's word, but it just "contains" God's Word; and that we need to interpret it according to the mores and culture of our day. I would like to suggest that Jesus' view is just the opposite. On the most important doctrine of His day and of our day—the resurrection—He uses one of the most obscure grammatical issues to make His point:

> Do not think that I have come to abolish the Law or the Prophets; I have not come to abolish them but to fulfill them. For truly I tell you, until heaven and earth disappear, not the smallest letter, not the least stroke of a pen, will by any means

67

disappear from the Law until everything is accomplished. (Matt. 5:17–18)

The smallest stroke and letter in Hebrew is a "yod" and looks like a reverse comma. The Hebrew letters *b* and *d* are very common, and only a thin, little stroke makes the difference between them. Jesus meant that every minute detail of God's Word, even the tiniest stroke, will be fulfilled.

Let's take a closer look at a couple examples of Jesus' attention to detail. There were two prominent religious groups who could not agree. The Sadducees, the theological liberals of their day, didn't believe in the resurrection, and the Pharisees, theological conservatives of their day, did. Both groups consistently tried to undermine Jesus' authority with their what-if scenarios in an attempt to trap Him. They hoped Jesus' answer would violate Jewish or Roman laws so they could have grounds to get rid of Him.

In Matthew 22 the what-if scenario went something like this: There was this man married to a woman and the man died. According to Jewish law, his brother was to marry the woman to provide offspring. After the second brother married her, he died before they could have any children. The same thing happened to all of the man's brothers. So basically the woman married eight brothers who all died and the woman never had any children. Then came the big question: Who would the woman be married to in the resurrection?

The Sadducees were baiting Jesus and trying to prove that the resurrection couldn't be true.

Jesus replied in Matthew 22:29–32,

You are in error because you do not know the Scriptures or the power of God. At the resurrection people will neither marry nor be given in marriage; they will be like the angels in heaven. But about the resurrection of the dead—have you not read what God said to you, "I am the God of Abraham, the God of Isaac, and the God of Jacob"? He is not the God of the dead but of the living.

Jesus addressed the Sadducees' and Pharisees' obvious question. At the resurrection, people will not marry or be given in marriage, but will be like the angels in heaven. Then He addressed what they were really thinking, and He used the words of God from the Old Testament, "But about the resurrection of the dead—have you not read what God said to you, 'I am the God of Abraham, the God of Isaac, and the God of Jacob'?"

Do you see what Jesus used as His foundation for the truth of the resurrection? It was the tense of a verb. I *am* instead of I *was*. Jesus believed the Old Testament revealed the breath of God. Theologians call this *verbal plenary inspiration*. Verbal: word. Plenary: every word. Inspiration: God-breathed. "I am the God of Abraham." In other words, Abraham is still alive, just not on the earth. Isaac is still alive. Jacob is still alive . . . "I am." Jesus proved the resurrection on the tense of a verb.

Jesus believed Scripture to be the words of God. If Jesus used Scripture and said that it is from God, then I don't feel anti-intellectual to be in His camp.

Conclusion

Before we continue our journey together, I'd like to ask you a question. What are your biggest issues with the Bible? What have you heard that has caused you to question the Bible's validity?

Maybe you're like me when my professor looked at me with disdain, as though I had thrown my brains in the trash to be a follower of Jesus. Or maybe you're like so many people that I meet who have unconsciously bought into the "who can trust a 2000-year-old book to give direction to their life" mentality, without ever having read it or studied its origin.

Jesus proved the resurrection on the tense of a verb.

The fact of the matter is that we trust documents all the time to give us direction. Our life is built around written records of truth, whether they be in science, literature, or medicine.

How do we validate those? Don't we dig into the past to find out if what they say is historically verifiable? Don't we check out the author and discover where he came from, his credibility, and what credible experts say?

I know of no other issue that will make a bigger difference in your life than having full confidence that you can trust that the Bible is the Word of God. And by trust, I mean making major life decisions that affect both time and eternity with no sense of feeling inferior or anti-intellectual. In the next chapter I will share with you the turning point in my journey with the Bible and why I have full confidence in it today.

I happen to be rather logical and analytical in my thinking. As a result, as I've stated before, I tend to be a skeptic. So believing that the Bible was actually God's Word was a big stretch for me. In the next chapter I will share the logical evidence that so overwhelmed me that it settled the issue once and for all and gave me an unshakable confidence that the Bible is in fact the Word of God.

4

Don't Take My Word for It

It was my junior year in college. I had been a Christian for about two and a half years and had developed the habit of reading the Bible and praying nearly every morning. I was a part of a college Christian ministry that was filled with zeal, love, and great relationships. My experience with Jesus in this new way of life brought great joy and a peace that I had never before experienced.

Life was great. I was on a basketball scholarship, had a pretty Christian girlfriend, was leading my first Bible study, and was "on fire for God." Then it happened—I had a crisis of faith. As I was reading the Bible one morning, a thought flashed through my mind: "What if all of this is just an emotional experience? What if this is just idealism run amok in an artificial college world? Can I really believe that what I'm

71

reading is true and that the God who made all that there is actually speaks through a book?"

Those thoughts deeply disturbed me. I tried to shake them off and tell myself that it was just the enemy. But for several weeks I continued to read with an attitude of skepticism. I looked for holes and logical inconsistencies, probing the Scriptures like someone kicking the tires of a car to see if they are really any good. My joy was replaced by doubt, and my newfound peace simply evaporated.

> I looked for holes and logical inconsistencies, probing the Scriptures like someone kicking the tires of a car.

The old skeptic was resurrected. I began to examine every relationship, every meeting, every song we sang from the viewpoint of a cynic. Is this mind manipulation? Is this delusional groupthink? I was miserable and had to find out in a way that would satisfy my intellectual criteria that I could really trust the Bible.

The turning point for me was the overwhelming evidence of prophecy and the undeniable supernatural transmission of the Scripture over thousands of years. Let's look at those things together.

Reason #6: Fulfilled Prophecy

As a young Christian, I didn't know much about the Bible and knew even less about Bible prophecy, yet as I looked for answers, I soon discovered that fulfilled prophecy sets the Bible apart from all other religious writings. Fulfilled prophecy was objective, not philosophical. Every bone in my skeptical body wanted proof. I think that prophecy (something said in advance that later happened) is powerful evidence that the Bible is, in fact, God's Word.

Have you ever enjoyed a fortune cookie after Chinese takeout? You break open the cookie, pop it in your mouth, and read your fortune. They usually say something positive, kind of like this . . . "A really amazingly good thing will happen to you sometime soon" or "You will meet someone very soon who will completely change your life for the better." The fortunes are so vague that I often can't help but laugh.

Prophecy is not a vague fortune cookie, it is detailed and specific. Prophecy is one of God's litmus tests that He used to prove He really is the One true God versus all the other religious claims. One hundred percent of the time, God accurately predicts, often in great detail, what will happen, hundreds and even thousands of years before it happens.

Throughout the book of Isaiah, we see God use prophecy as proof of His authority. The children of Israel were not doing well, and they put their hope for the future in idols they made with their own hands. God challenged the children of Israel to put their trust in the One who could accurately foretell the future. Who would it be? Israel's idols or God Himself?

> Remember the former things, those of long ago;
> I am God, and there is no other;
> I am God, and there is none like me.
> I make known the end from the beginning,
> from ancient times, what is still to come.
> I say, "My purpose will stand,
> and I will do all that I please." (Isa. 46:9–10)

God said, I am the One true God. Yahweh. "I make known the end from the beginning, from ancient times, what is still to come" is kind of a poetic way to say, *I know the end from the beginning,* and notice He said, "My purpose will stand, and I will do all that I please."

Let's take a look at a few biblical prophecies and see if what God foretold really came to pass. The first biblical prophecy I would like to examine is important, because it is so specific and appears improbable, even impossible, that it could happen.

First, the judgment of the ancient city of Tyre. Ezekiel's prophecy in chapter 26 included five points:

1. Nebuchadnezzar would besiege and absolutely destroy the city.
2. Multiple nations would come against it.
3. The ruins would be scraped from the site and thrown into the sea.
4. The site would become a place for fishermen to spread their nets.
5. The city would never be rebuilt again.

The city of Tyre was one of the biggest and most powerful and successful cities of the early seventh century—like our modern cities of San Francisco, Hong Kong, Sydney, Los Angeles, or New York. For Tyre to be completely destroyed and never rebuilt was unimaginable.

Let's see what happened to Tyre. Nebuchadnezzar, king of Babylon, attacked the city for thirteen years. With all his wealth and supplies to back his campaign, he decimated the city and turned it to rubble. During this time, the wealthy and the powerful people of Tyre escaped about a half mile outside of the original city to an island. It became the new fortified city of Tyre. Nebuchadnezzar decided that he had done enough and left.

If I was reading that prophecy, I would think to myself that God was close, but He didn't get it quite right. The prophecy was not completely fulfilled at that time. But wait, there is more to come.

Three hundred years later, about 322 BC, Alexander the Great was determined to take over as much of the entire world as he could. On his march to Egypt, he got to the powerful city of Tyre and decided that Tyre was a threat that must be destroyed. He used his small fleet to attack the huge fortress of Tyre, but because they were using catapults, he realized his methods were not going to be successful.

For three years he paused his larger campaign, and his soldiers built a causeway a half mile from the shore all the way to the city and focused their fighting power on Tyre. When the siege was done, Alexander the Great completely decimated the city. Nothing was left. To this day, the original city of Tyre is just a flat, barren piece of rock where fishermen dry their nets. You can still see the remains of the causeway his soldiers built. And although another city was renamed Tyre, that original city has never been rebuilt. God's accuracy rate was 100 percent.

Let's look at another prophecy. This one is about the succession of world empires found in the book of Daniel.

Most of us have heard the story of Daniel in the lions' den but don't understand the man behind the story. After Israel's disobedience, the Babylonians invaded Israel in 586 BC and Daniel was taken captive to Babylon.

Daniel's time in Babylon spanned three dynasties. He knew God promised to bring His people back together, but after so many years, he wondered when it would actually happen. In response to Daniel's prayer, God gave Daniel an image of a statue. God showed Daniel the four major empires of the world over the next several hundred years. Each empire was represented by a different building material in a different location of the large statue (Dan. 2).

The empires in order were the Babylonians, the Medo-Persians, the Greeks, then the Romans. Daniel's prophecy concerning the Greek era was especially interesting, as it outlined a ruler with a worldwide kingdom that would later be divided into four parts. That person would be Alexander the Great, whose empire was divided and given to his four generals.

God described specific kingdoms and what they would be like hundreds of years before they rose to power.

As a young Christian, I began to read through these prophecies in the Bible, and the more I read, the more convinced I became of the supernatural nature of the Bible.

As amazing as these prophecies are, I believe the most astounding prophecies are about Christ. There are over three hundred specific prophecies of Jesus' first coming. They describe who He would be, what would happen to Him, where

He would be born, and much more. These detailed prophecies were made hundreds, and in some cases, thousands of years before He was born.

These are just thirty of the over three hundred prophecies about Jesus:

> The most astounding prophecies are about Christ. There are over three hundred specific prophecies of Jesus' first coming.

1. He would be born of a woman (Gen. 3:15).
2. He would be born of a virgin (Isa. 7:14).
3. He would be a descendent of Abraham (Gen. 12:3; 18:18).
4. He would be from the tribe of Judah (Gen. 49:10).
5. He would be from the house of David (Ps. 132:11; Jer. 23:5; 33:15; Isa. 11:10).
6. He would be born in Bethlehem (Mic .5:2).
7. There would be a forerunner who would prepare the way (Isa. 40:3–5).
8. He would be anointed with the Holy Spirit (Isa. 11:2).
9. He would have a preaching ministry (Isa. 61:1–2).
10. He would speak in parables (Ps. 78:2).
11. He would have a healing ministry (Isa. 35:5–6).
12. He would be a prophet (Deut. 18:15, 19).
13. He would also function as a priest (Ps. 110:4).
14. The time of His appearance was foretold (Dan. 9:24–26).
15. His death was foretold (Ps. 22; Ps. 69:21).
16. He would have a triumphal entry on a donkey (Zech. 9:9).

17. He would be betrayed for thirty pieces of silver (Zech. 11:12–13).

18. He would remain silent before His accusers (Isa. 53:7).

19. He would be abandoned by His disciples (Zech. 13:7).

20. He would be beaten (Isa. 50:6).

21. He would be spat upon (Isa. 50:6).

22. He would be mocked (Isa. 50:6).

23. His hands and feet would be pierced (Ps. 22:6).

24. He would be crucified with transgressors (Isa. 53:12).

25. Lots would be cast for His garments (Ps. 22:18).

26. He would cry out from the cross (Ps. 22:1).

27. None of His bones would be broken (Ps. 22:17; Exod. 12:46; Ps. 34:20).

28. He would be buried with the rich (Isa. 53:9).

29. He would be resurrected (Ps. 16:10).

30. He would be exalted (Ps. 110:1).

Peter Stoner was the chairman of the department of mathematics and astronomy at Pasadena City College. He later went on to teach and have the same role at Westmont College. Being a mathematician, he wanted to know the probability of eight fulfilled prophecies. He figured out that the probability of any man fulfilling eight prophecies would be one in ten to the seventeenth power. That's 1 in 100,000,000,000,000,000! He knew that a number might not mean that much to us, so he gave us this picture to help us comprehend this staggering probability.

Fulfilling eight prophecies would be like covering the entire state of Texas in silver dollars two feet deep. Now mark one of these silver dollars and stir the whole mass thoroughly. Blindfold a man and tell him he can travel as far as he wishes, but he must pick up one silver dollar and say that it is the right one. What chance would he have of getting the right one? Just the same chance that the prophets would have had writing eight prophecies and have all of them come true in any one man.[1]

Jesus didn't just fulfill eight prophecies, He fulfilled three hundred. This was the kind of objective proof that quieted my doubts about the Bible. Even as a skeptic, I could no longer stare at these facts and just say, "Wow." I had to make a decision about the trustworthiness of the Bible, and I did. Fulfilled prophecy is among the strongest of evidences that the Bible is God's Word and that we can trust what it says.

God is all-knowing, He is all-powerful, and He can preserve His Word. There are more prophecies to be fulfilled. We are living in prophetic times.

Reason #7: Transmission

The seventh reason I believe that the Bible is the very Word of God is transmission. The Bible's purity and preservation throughout the centuries is nothing short of miraculous.

Do you remember the kids' game telephone? You get nine or ten children together and the first one says, "Go outside and get the dog." They whisper this to one another down the line until it gets to the tenth kid. By the tenth time the message is passed along, it has completely changed to, "The girl in the yellow dress looks like a hog." In all the times we played, I don't think the message ever stayed the same. It always changed in the retelling.

I have often been asked, "Can a Bible that has been copied so many times for so many hundreds of years really be accurate?" Without the ability to copy and paste or make a quick trip to FedEx for copies, how were biblical copies made? Let's dig into the answer together.

As I learned about the job of a scribe, my understanding about Bible transmission became much clearer. A scribe would take an original copy and very carefully write letter by letter. As a scribe wrote each letter down, they would form into rows. The copied letters and rows would then be checked to assure that the scribe had matched the original copy. A random letter and row would be selected to be matched to the original. They could have counted seven across and eleven down—was it the same letter as the original? What about thirty letters across and twenty-five down? If the answer was yes, the scribe would move on. If the answer was no, the copy would be destroyed and the scribe would start over.

When an Old Testament scribe came to the place in the text where the name of God needed to be written, the scribe would only use four letters (YHWH), because the name of God, Yahweh or Jehovah, was so holy it was never pronounced and never fully written out. After writing the four letters for the name of God, a scribe would go ceremonially wash before coming back to write again. This was done every time a scribe wrote the name of God. The level of focus and meticulous copying ensured an extremely high percentage of accuracy.

The proximity of the manuscripts is another way to check for accuracy. If you want to check a document from antiquity, you ask: When was it written? What's the earliest copy we have? And how many copies of the manuscript do we have? These copies are then checked with one another for consistency and any possible errors.

Let me give you some documents from antiquity for comparison. Plato lived between 427 to 347 BC. Our earliest copy of his work is AD 900. There are twelve hundred years between his writing and our first copy. There are seven copies of his work.

Aristotle lived between 384 to 322 BC and the earliest copy we have of his work is AD 1100. That's a fourteen-hundred-year difference, but we have forty-nine copies.

Homer, circa 900 BC, is famous for his works *The Iliad* and *The Odyssey*. Our earliest copy is 400 BC, so there are about five hundred years between the time he lived and the earliest copies. We have over six hundred copies of Homer's work. No one doubts the authenticity of Plato, Aristotle, or Homer.

Now let's look at the New Testament. The New Testament was written between AD 40 and AD 100, and the earliest copied portion is from AD 125. That is only a twenty-five-year difference. In those twenty-five years, people were still alive to authenticate the text. In total there are 24,643 hand-written portions or complete copies of the New Testament.

The Bible is the most accurately transmitted ancient document on the face of the earth. In fact, when the Dead Sea

Scrolls were found in 1947, the telephone game theory got completely blown out as conjecture or objection.

> **The Bible is the most accurately transmitted ancient document on the face of the earth.**

The Dead Sea Scrolls provide further evidence that the Bible is an accurate document. Dating from the third century BC to the first century AD, the scrolls contain partial or complete copies of every book of the Old Testament except Esther and multiple copies of Deuteronomy, Psalms, and Isaiah. The first scrolls were discovered by a Bedouin goatherd in 1947, and by 1956 all the scrolls were found in a total of eleven caves. The amazing thing is that they are over a thousand years older than previously identified biblical manuscripts, and yet over 95 percent of the wording is the same. The only differences are variations in spelling and punctuation. There are no theological differences between the scrolls and our modern translations. The Bible is an accurate document that can be trusted.[2]

The Dead Sea Scrolls, almost fifty thousand texts, revealed that the Old Testament was not degraded over time. God spoke it, it was copied, and the text we have today is the same text that people read well over two thousand years ago. God transmitted His Word to you and me in a supernatural way. When you read the Bible, you are reading the Word of God.

Proximity of Manuscripts

Author	Time Written	Earliest Copy	Time Span	# of copies
Plato	399–347 BC	AD 900	1,200 years	7
Aristotle	342–322 BC	AD 1100	1,400 years	49
Homer	ca. 900 BC	400 BC	500 years	643
New Testament	AD 40–100	AD 125	25 years	24,000

Reason #8: Impact

The final reason I believe the Bible is God's Word is more experiential, but it is extraordinarily powerful. The reason is the very impact of the Bible. Its power to transform lives and nations is overwhelming. Wherever the Word of God goes, it brings life, health, and vitality. Despite those who have twisted its meaning to manipulate, control, or gain financially, the history of the Bible's impact past and present is staggering.

Throughout history, there are individuals who responded to God's Word and made a huge difference in the world. William Wilberforce played a significant role in eradicating slavery in England. Lord Ashley Cooper helped bring an end to abusive child labor in factories and mines. Open the Bible and read it for yourself. Where the Bible is believed and lived out, women become *persons* instead of *property*. Where the Bible is believed and lived out, equal rights and justice are championed. Where the Bible is believed and lived out, slavery is not an option because the dignity of humanity and the truth of Scripture wins. Where the Bible is believed and lived out, people are loved and needs are met.

The Bible has certainly had macro impact in the world for good. But what has amazed me personally and in my teaching for over thirty years is the power of God's Word to change an individual's life. When I was going through my deepest doubts about God and the Bible, there were two things I could not dismiss: the objective prophetic record that is undeniable and accurate, and the actual changes that had occurred in my own life.

After reading the Bible for a few weeks as a new Christian, my foul mouth was supernaturally cleaned up. I did not try to stop cursing or making lewd remarks, but I noticed about three weeks into my new life that they had simply disappeared. Little did I know then that the Bible makes a promise about itself and the transformation of individual lives: "Do not conform to the pattern of this world, but be transformed by the renewing of your mind. Then you will be able to test and approve what God's will is—his good, pleasing and perfect will" (Rom. 12:2).

I couldn't help but notice after two years of reading the Bible that my deep insecurities that had manifested themselves in an arrogant attitude, always seeking to impress, and lack of concern for others had been replaced with quiet confidence, growing humility, and a genuine concern for the needs of others.

Jesus promised that if we would take in the truth of God's Word and apply it to our lives, we would be free. "Then you will know the truth, and the truth will set you free" (John 8:32). I have had the joy and privilege of watching that happen in thousands of lives—addictions broken, eating disorders healed, sexual abuse stopped, workaholism transformed, marriages restored, and peace and power replacing anxiety and fear. I have received thousands of emails as I teach God's Word through Living on the Edge. This one I recently received out of the blue from a person I've never met is so powerful:

Mr. Ingram,

I am a dedicated listener and wanted to thank you for having such a positive impact in my life. Without writing

84

a novel, I have been a believer of Christ since as long as I remember. But I don't think I've been a "liver" of Christ until about 8 months ago. By purely the grace of God, I was driving home from work in my usual one-hour commute and listening to some filthy comedy on Sirius radio. I thought to myself that God doesn't want me to do this. I searched the Sirius program and found your show. It was the series "Good to Great in God's Eyes." I was immediately drawn in and have been a listener, reader, supporter and follower ever since. So much so, I am sure my wife is tired of hearing me say, "Chip says . . ."

But mostly, with all due respect, it isn't about you. It is about how you introduced me to a new relationship with God. Thanks to your suggestions, I spend time with God every morning first reading the Daily Walk Bible, then reading "something great" and then spending time in prayer. I have started to memorize scripture and feel a change in me.

I am a lawyer and have a busy, stressful life. I deal with the worst of people in so many ways. But knowing God is there for me makes it all okay. And I hope to show the light of Christ in my interactions with people. I know I am a better, happier person because of my new relationship with God. I know I am a horrible sinner (the worst I know) but I know my redemption is through Christ, I know God loves me, and I know He is in control.

I know you didn't do any of these things, but you just pushed me in the right direction. I want to give you a heartfelt thank you for guiding me in this way. I appreciate you more than these words could express.

> *Thank you and God bless you*
> *and your family,*
> *Matt Batezel, Cypress, California*

Conclusion

Our journey through the last two chapters has been an amazing one. The Bible truly is a unique and extraordinary book. I have shared eight reasons why I believe the Bible is the Word of God, and I encourage you to further explore the Bible for yourself. Coming to a solid conviction about the Bible was a significant turning point in my life, and it can be for you as well.

Below, I leave you with a challenge. Depending on where you are in your personal journey, one of these will apply to you.

For the doubting Christian: These two chapters are critical to your growth. As it becomes more unpopular to be a follower of Christ, our beliefs must move to convictions. Consider digging into an area of doubt concerning the Bible or the resurrection and do some personal study and research for yourself.

For the honest skeptic: Examine the evidence in these two chapters with an open mind. Don't take my word for it or buy what others have told you. Then commit to read the four Gospels—Matthew, Mark, Luke, and John—to discover firsthand who Jesus is. You owe it to yourself to interact personally and honestly explore the Jesus of the New Testament.

For the new believer: Get in the Word of God on a regular basis. It will bring life to your soul. There are multiple Bible reading plans available on the YouVersion mobile app. Choose one that most fits your needs and begin to develop a daily habit of Bible reading and prayer.

For the mature believer: Go to the next level and memorize some Scripture. I highly recommend the Topical Memory System by the Navigators. For a bigger challenge, take a chapter like Romans 12 or Psalm 23 and memorize it and review it daily for thirty days.

Additional Resources:

Erwin W. Lutzer, *Seven Reasons Why You Can Trust the Bible*

ChristianAnswers.Net, *How Do We Know the Bible Is True?* http://christiananswers.net/q-eden/edn-t003.html

Norman L. Geisler and William E. Nix, *From God to Us: How We Got Our Bible*

Joseph M. Holden and Norman Geisler, *The Popular Handbook of Archaeology and the Bible: Discoveries that Confirm the Reliability of Scripture*

Alfred Hoerth, *Archaeology and the Old Testament*

Craig Blomberg, *The Historical Reliability of the Gospels*

Craig Blomberg, *Can We Still Believe the Bible?*

Navigators, *Topical Memory System*

YouVersion mobile app

Chip Ingram app

5

Why I Believe in Life after Death

I will never forget the first time that it happened to me. I was a young pastor and had been talking to one of our church member's friends. I didn't know all the details, but it was obvious that he was really down on God and really down on the church. He was involved in a dark movement whose followers focused on death, wore black all the time, and were adamantly against God, the Bible, and the church.

In some conversations about spiritual things with his friend, I heard phrases like, "There is no God, we live, we die, and that's it! We're just like the animals, and when you die, you return to dust. I don't believe in God, I don't believe in life after death, and I don't believe in the church"—all said with more than just a little emotion.

Sometime later, a young man from our church who lost his way for a season became involved with the group. He was one of those kids everybody liked and had that wow factor about him that made him the center of every social relationship. A drug addiction eventually led him to rehab and restoration with his family and the Lord. Tragically, in a moment of weakness, he overdosed on heroin and died a few days later. I found myself doing a funeral in our church with about forty of his friends from this dark movement, all dressed in black, attending the service.

One by one these teenagers got up and spoke with love and affection about their friend. And then something very strange occurred—they talked about him being at peace and being in a better place. Out of the blue, and in complete contrast to their intellectual arguments, were comments about a positive afterlife and seeing him again out of his misery and struggle with drug addiction.

That was many years ago and I've watched this phenomenon many times since. You see, it's one thing to intellectually argue against an afterlife, but something deep inside us happens when someone we love dies. The thought of no hope, of finality, of separation forever challenges the very core of our being.

One of the most important questions we don't ask very often is, what happens when we die? What actually happens when we take our last breath, our heart stops, and the brain waves are completely flat? What occurs?

Is it intellectually feasible to believe that there is life after death? What do you believe will happen to you when you die? Why? What does the Scripture say? What did Jesus and the Bible teach about what happens to people after they die?

Since 100 percent of the human race will die, this is a really important question for all of us to answer. I want to share with you in this chapter why I believe there is life after death. I want to journey together with you and examine the case for life after death.

What actually happens when we take our last breath, our heart stops, and the brain waves are completely flat?

I would like to introduce our journey on this topic by reviewing six indicators from various disciplines that make a compelling argument that there is life after death. The question is, what really happens? Is it possible to know while living in this life what the next life holds?

The answer is yes, and for good reason. We know that the Bible and what it says about Jesus is reliable. In addition, Jesus talks very specifically about what happens to us after we die. And having been resurrected from the dead as the Son of God, He is an authority on the subject. But before we explore what Jesus and the Bible teach about the afterlife, let's look at six strong indicators that there actually is some kind of existence after our physical death.

Six Strong Indicators of Life after Death

1. Nature

The pattern and the cycle of nature provide us with evidence that there is more than this life. Watching colorful, spring flowers appear from winter's cold, hard ground gives us a picture that winter is not the end. When seeds fall to the ground and die, they bring forth new life. The caterpillar creates a cocoon that it stays in until it is ready to emerge in its new life as a butterfly.

Plato is often quoted as writing, "There's a cycle in nature that is obvious to us all. I'm not sure what's after death, but nature seems to give us a picture of what it will be like. Some kind of new life after death."

2. Anthropology

When we look at humanity across time, of all backgrounds and all religions, what do we find? Anthropologists say that every culture on earth, from those who live in primitive parts of the Amazon, to the Himalayas, to urban cultures, all believe in some kind of afterlife. Most societies treat death not as an end into nothingness, but as a transition into some unknown state. It seems that there is something built into the human soul that not only transcends culture, but intuitively knows that physical death is a door, not a dead end.

3. Psychology

In fact, there is a common thread for all human beings in that we innately think there is more than this physical life—the sense of "there's got to be something more." The hunger and thirst for meaning and significance that is never quite satisfied.

We see it in the pyramids built by the Egyptians, or in the Greeks putting coins in the mouths of their buried so they could pay the ferry man at the River Styx. For some it is seeking that paradise level or achieving the virtue of goodness before death. People often have a sense that there needs to be a reconciling of good and evil. There's a weight that we feel down deep inside our hearts that after we die, there must be more.

C. S. Lewis logically deduces in *Mere Christianity*, "If I find in myself a desire which no experience in this world can satisfy, the most probable explanation is that I was made for another world."[1] The writer of Ecclesiastes put it this way in chapter 3 when he said that God has placed eternity in our hearts (v. 11). We are made for something longer and deeper than this world can ever provide.

4. Ethics

You have probably noticed that the world is not fair. Good things happen to bad people, and bad things happen to good people. The rationale for an afterlife from ethics goes something like this: to have morality, there needs to be justice and fairness. Evil must be punished and good must be rewarded. Yet when we look at our world, we see people do really bad things and yet good seems to happen to them, at least for a season. By contrast we've all known people who seem to be honest, kind, and loving and yet they suffer abuse, get hit by a drunk driver, or experience a premature death. The argument from ethics states that an afterlife is essential for life to be fair, because good must ultimately be rewarded and evil must be punished—if not in this life, then in the next.

5. Philosophy

The argument for an afterlife from philosophy really takes the ethical argument and makes the logical deduction that if life has to be fair and it's not fair in this life, then an afterlife is required to balance the scales of justice. Justice doesn't always occur in this life, so there has to be another time of judgment or reconciliation of good and evil.

Immanuel Kant took the reasoning of ethics and basically said, "If there is a good God and there is morality, there has to be an afterlife for any of life to make sense."

Psalm 9:7–8 says, "The Lord reigns forever; he has established his throne for judgment. He rules the world in righteousness and judges the peoples with equity."

6. Science and Near-Death Experiences

If you have been to the movies recently or downloaded a best-seller, you have probably noticed that near-death stories are very popular. People want to know what comes after life here on earth. Millions of books have been sold by those claiming they have died and experienced what life is like after one dies. Although their accounts vary widely, let's take a look at the research on near-death experiences.

> Nearly 40 percent experienced some form of awareness during the time they had been declared dead.

In 2014, the largest medical research study ever conducted on cardiac arrest patients was released. The UK-based team spent four years analyzing survivors' interviews; nearly 40 percent experienced some form of awareness during the time they had been declared dead. The experts' currently held belief is that once the heart stops beating, the brain ceases functioning within twenty to thirty seconds and awareness is no longer possible. The results of this study contradicts this belief.[2]

The research, published in the *Journal of Resuscitation*, included 2,060 patients in fifteen hospitals in the US, Australia, and the United Kingdom. Of those who survived their cardiac arrest, 46 percent experienced a broad range of mental recollections, 9 percent had what was called a "classical near-death experience," and 2 percent had an out-of-body experience after death where they reported being able to see themselves and describe what the doctors were doing. They were also able to recall jokes that were said, specific events that happened in the room, and other facts that would be impossible for them to know.

Dr. Parnia said, "The findings of the study as a whole suggested that the recalled experience surrounding death now merits further genuine investigation without prejudice."[3]

Not one of the above six indicators necessarily proves that there is life after death. But if I were a skeptic, which I can be, I think that their combined impact makes for a strong case that this life is not all there is. Which raises the question, what happens after we die? We demonstrated that Jesus is an authority on the subject because He's the author of life and has come back from the dead. We've also established that the Bible is a supernatural document that is trustworthy. So let's examine what Jesus and the Bible clearly teach about what happens to us immediately after we die.

> The combined impact of these indicators makes for a strong case that this life is not all there is.

Jesus and the Bible on Life after Death

As a follower of Christ, I think the greatest evidence for life after death is Jesus. He is the ultimate authority on the subject because He is the only person who came from heaven, died, and came back to life. On our journey through the evidence of the resurrection, we learned that Jesus appeared to people for forty days in His resurrected body, with over five hundred eyewitnesses in twelve different locations. Thousands of people witnessed the resurrected Christ and His miracles.

So what did Jesus teach about what happens to us after we die? Is there a literal heaven? Is there a literal hell? One minute after we die, what will happen? And what will be the basis of our eternal existence? Does the Bible address these issues clearly and in a way that ordinary people like ourselves can understand?

The Scripture has much to say about what happens after we die. There are specific details that concern believers, unbelievers, nations, judgments, and even events that lead to Christ's return. For our purposes, however, I want to pull back the lens of perspective and look at the bigger picture. So let's dive into this critical question by summarizing the teaching of the Bible into four overarching truths that the Scripture clearly teaches.

> *Truth #1: At death, every person's soul or spirit enters immediately and consciously into the relational aspects of eternal existence.*

You might want to read that sentence above one more time. The words are chosen carefully and they have very significant meaning. What I mean to say is that the immaterial part of us—the real you, not your physical body but your soul or spirit—will upon death be immediately conscious of your new existence. You will not have some protracted sleep in the grave. You will not be in some ethereal limbo and wondering where you are or what's going on. You will not be alone but will be able to recognize and relate to others who have died.

Jesus' Paradigm of the Afterlife

These are the very points Jesus makes when He gives us a sneak peek into the afterlife in the parable He taught in Luke 16:19–29:

> The time came when the beggar died and the angels carried him to Abraham's side. The rich man also died and was buried. In Hades, where he was in torment, he looked up and saw Abraham far away, with Lazarus by his side. So he called to him, "Father Abraham, have pity on me and send Lazarus to dip the tip of his finger in water and cool my tongue, because I am in agony in this fire."
>
> But Abraham replied, "Son, remember that in your lifetime you received your good things, while Lazarus received bad things, but now he is comforted here and you are in agony. And besides all this, between us and you a great chasm has been set in place, so that those who want to go from here to you cannot, nor can anyone cross over from there to us."
>
> He answered, "Then I beg you, father, send Lazarus to my family, for I have five brothers. Let him warn them, so that they will not also come to this place of torment."
>
> Abraham replied, "They have Moses and the Prophets; let them listen to them."

In other words, they've got the Word of God.

"'No, Father Abraham,' he said, 'but if someone from the dead goes to them, they will repent'" (v. 30). Jesus then gives them another peek into the future when He says, "If they do not listen to Moses and the Prophets, they will not be convinced even if someone rises from the dead" (v. 31). Can you imagine the response? And yet He knew exactly what would happen and how people would respond.

The paradigm is simply this: Hades is the place where the spirits of the wicked are prior to resurrection. Paradise is a place in the presence of God, for those who have not yet been resurrected. Later we will learn that one day everyone will be resurrected. Jesus gives a clear picture that both men have a conscious awareness. There is a fixed chasm, and once a person dies, there is no second chance.

Paul's Paradigm of the Afterlife

The apostle Paul, in 2 Corinthians 5, would use a different metaphor. He talks about our bodies being a tent. Paul tells us with assurance that there is a place for us after we die. I encourage you to read the following passage slowly for yourself:

> For we know that if the earthly tent we live in is destroyed, we have a building from God, an eternal house in heaven, not built by human hands. Meanwhile we groan, longing to be clothed instead with our heavenly dwelling, because when we are clothed, we will not be found naked. For while we are in this tent, we groan and are burdened, because we do not wish to be unclothed but to be clothed instead with our heavenly dwelling, so that what is mortal may be swallowed up by life. Now the one who has fashioned us for this very

purpose is God, who has given us the Spirit as a deposit, guaranteeing what is to come.

Therefore we are always confident and know that as long as we are at home in the body we are away from the Lord. For we live by faith, not by sight. We are confident, I say, and would prefer to be away from the body and at home with the Lord. (vv. 1–8)

Paul makes the same point concerning what happens immediately after we die. He says to be absent from the body is to be at home with the Lord. In Philippians 1, the apostle is between the rock and the hard place. He thinks he is going to be executed as he writes to the Philippian church, "I don't know what to do. To be with Christ is very much better but maybe I should stay because I am required to do more ministry." But Paul's expectation and view were clear. He understood that the moment he died, his spirit would be in the presence of God.

I am torn between the two: I desire to depart and be with Christ, which is better by far; but it is more necessary for you that I remain in the body. Convinced of this, I know that I will remain, and I will continue with all of you for your progress and joy in the faith, so that through my being with you again your boasting in Christ Jesus will abound on account of me. (Phil. 1:23–26)

Truth #2: Every person will one day be resurrected and live forever.

I was a Christian for years before the reality of this truth dawned on me. I knew that believers would be resurrected, but never thought about the fact that everyone will be resurrected.

In Acts 24 the apostle Paul was on trial and giving his defense. He told everyone present that he was not changing Judaism, but he was following the Messiah who came to fulfill Judaism. Listen to his words.

> However, I admit that I worship the God of our ancestors as a follower of the Way, which they call a sect. I believe everything that is in accordance with the Law and that is written in the Prophets, and I have the same hope in God as these men themselves have, that there will be a resurrection of **both the righteous and the wicked.** (Acts 24:14–15, emphasis added)

Paul made an interesting statement in this passage. As a follower of the Way, he worshiped the God of his fathers and shared the same hope of resurrection as the Pharisees who were accusing him. Paul clearly understood that everyone would be resurrected and everyone would live forever.

This next passage gives us a picture of the Great White Throne of the ultimate judgment. There will be a resurrection of the righteous and a resurrection of the wicked. All of humanity will be resurrected.

> Then I saw a great white throne and him who was seated on it. The earth and the heavens fled from his presence, and there was no place for them. And I saw the dead, great and small, standing before the throne, and books were opened. Another book was opened, which is the book of life. The dead were judged according to what they had done as recorded in the books. The sea gave up the dead that were in it, and death and Hades gave up the dead that were in them, and each person was judged according to what they had done. (Rev. 20:11–13)

Truth #3: *Every person will be judged and granted the extended capacity to fulfill in eternity the deepest yearnings and desires of their hearts while on earth.*

Let's unpack Truth #3 phrase by phrase.

First, every person will be judged. Believers and nonbelievers will be judged, and we will all have to give an account to God. I will explain this in more detail in just a moment. This judgment will then result in giving every person "extended capacity" to fulfill forever their deepest yearnings and desires with regard to their relationship with Christ. Those who received God's forgiveness during their lifetime and longed to know Him and serve Him will be given the extended capacity to do that at a depth and level unimaginable for all eternity in heaven with Christ. Those who stiff-armed God, rejected His grace, and didn't want anything to do with Him will be given an extended capacity to live apart from God's presence forever.

The church doesn't talk much about judgment these days, but the Bible has much to say about it, and the chief spokesman on the topic is Jesus Himself. Interestingly, even apart from Scripture it seems that God has planted in the human heart a deep awareness of judgment and accountability.

I read a white paper recently by a cultural anthropologist whose goal was to look beyond all the different cultures and religions to find what it is about the human psyche that we all have in common. According to the anthropologist, every culture and every religion has a sense of "ought." Interestingly, everyone has a sense that there will be a day when you will give an account for all you have done. There will be judgment, a day of reckoning, of accountability.[4]

> God has planted in the human heart a deep awareness of judgment and accountability.

It's way bigger than an annual review. It's the review of your whole life. There are many different views of how this review will go. According to the Bible, "People are destined to die once, and after that to face judgment" (Heb. 9:27). There's not a second chance or a soul sleep. There's not an opportunity to see how everything comes out and then decide.

Every single person will be present for evaluation time. I'm very grateful that Jesus is the Judge. John 5 makes it very clear that He is the Judge. He alone was entrusted with the responsibility of being fully God and fully man. He lived on earth and was tempted in every way like us, but without sin. He cares so deeply for us and understands our struggles. He will be the Judge and He judges with absolute fairness.

> Very truly I tell you, whoever hears my word and believes him who sent me has eternal life and will not be judged but has crossed over from death to life. Very truly I tell you, a time is coming and has now come when the dead will hear the voice of the Son of God and those who hear will live. For as the Father has life in himself, so he has granted the Son also to have life in himself. And he has given him authority to judge because he is the Son of Man. Do not be amazed at this, for a time is coming when all who are in their graves will hear his voice. (John 5:24–28)

Jesus is fair, loving, and kind. No one will get a raw deal. People will not be judged by their intentions or by their own sense of morality but by their works. God's holiness demands that we are 100 percent pure in every relationship and area of our life in order to have fellowship with Him. The Bible is equally clear that no one measures up—"all have sinned and fall short of the glory of God" (Rom. 3:23). The consequences of our sin are universal.

> For the wages of sin is death, but the free gift of God is eternal life in Christ Jesus our Lord. (Rom. 6:23 NASB)

In John 5:24–28, Jesus clearly states that He is not only our judge but that He also came to save us, to forgive us, to actually cover our sin and take it upon Himself so that we might be made holy and acceptable to God. Note the amazing promise in verse 24: "Whoever hears my word and believes him who sent me **has eternal life**" (emphasis added). Eternal life is the life of Christ. It's not something that happens after we die, but it is a quality of life we received as a gift when we put our faith in Christ. Then notice the very next phrase; it says that we do not come into judgment but have passed from death to life.

God's heart's desire is that every person would acknowledge that Christ is the free gift of God so that they might have eternal relationships with Him forever. The Scripture emphatically states, "Here is a trustworthy saying that deserves full acceptance: Christ Jesus came into the world to save sinners" (1 Tim. 1:15).

Take a moment and ponder this statement: "In eternity you get an 'extended capacity' to fulfill the deepest yearnings and longings of your heart." In other words, what you really wanted and longed for on earth, you will get to experience more deeply and forever.

For example, there will be an extended capacity for intimacy with God for the people who follow Him, embrace forgiveness in Christ, and yearn to be close to Him. Have you ever had a moment when you have been in prayer and it seemed like you could reach out and touch God? Have there been times when He has whispered so loudly to you, it was like an audible voice? Maybe there have been times when you have experienced and felt God's love in ways you never had before. That is a small taste of what heaven will be like. You will experience an extended capacity for love, peace, and joy that is exponentially greater and infinitely deeper than anything you've experienced on earth.

You have gifts, dreams, and desires, and you will have an expanded capacity to use them and develop them forever in a perfect environment. Your relationship with Christ covers all your sin, and at the moment of death you'll be ushered into heaven. There you will have an expanded capacity, far beyond what you had on earth, to fulfill your yearnings and desire to know God, please God, honor Him, and follow Him in a new reality in a new heaven and new earth in a perfect environment.

By contrast, there are people who have spent most of their lives stiff-arming God. In their hearts, they tell God to leave them alone and not mess with their life. They don't want his morality or direction because they want to be in control. At the heart of turning away from God is our desire to worship ourselves.

If the deepest yearnings of a person's heart while on earth were all about themselves, their control, and their desire to have distance from God, they will receive just that. God is righteous, and He honors the dignity of our free choices. Every person who rejects God's offer of life with Him will have an extended capacity to be absolutely autonomous and alone forever.

> God is righteous, and He honors the dignity of our free choices.

Truth #4: Every person will spend eternity in heaven with Christ and fellow believers or in hell separated from God forever.

The Scripture is emphatically clear about the reality of heaven and hell. In recent days, some evangelical leaders have challenged the idea of hell. Although I'm certain they are well intentioned, their teaching flies in the face of the most just and loving Person who's ever lived—Jesus. Listen to Jesus' own words:

> Then they will go away and enter eternal punishment, but the righteous to eternal life. (Matt. 25:46)

Let me pause at this moment and say, nothing could be more important to you personally than knowing for certain of your relationship and eternal salvation through Jesus Christ. As a pastor for over thirty years, I continually meet people in excellent Bible-believing churches who are unclear about the gospel and uncertain about their eternal destiny.

Despite hearing the truth, they think that their "good deeds will somehow outweigh their bad deeds" and merit them eternal life. Others seem to have come to the conclusion that being religious, being nice, and going to church is the ticket to eternal life. Let me say as strongly as I can: *Eternal life is a gift that is received by faith, solely through the grace and work of Jesus Christ on your behalf, as He personally paid for your sin by dying in your place and for your sin on the cross. It must be personally received, and you can know for certain that you have it.*

Listen again to the very words of Jesus to you personally:

> Very truly I tell you, whoever *hears* my word and *believes* him who sent Me *has* eternal life and will not be judged but has crossed over from death to life. (John 5:24, emphasis added)

Read John 5:24 again and notice the tense of the verb, "has" eternal life. Eternal life isn't something you get after you die. It's a present possession that comes out of a relationship of receiving the forgiveness of God. The Spirit of God comes into your life and you are taken from the kingdom of darkness into the kingdom of light. It's a picture of Jesus being a bridge and those who trust and believe in Him are carried over the bridge. His payment covers our sin.

> Yet to all who did receive him, to those who believed in his name, he gave the right to become children of God. (John 1:12)

So before we continue and talk about why a loving God would create a place like hell, let me ask you if you have ever personally received Christ. Have you turned from your sin and with the empty hands of faith asked Christ to forgive you and come into your life? If not, I invite you to do that right now. (See video at www.livingontheedge.org/gospel.)

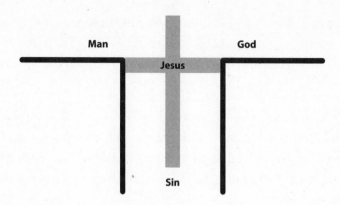

Why There Has to Be a Hell

Now let's tackle that difficult issue of hell. People often ask, "What kind of a loving God would send people into a fiery hell?" That question is usually followed by, "If that's how God is, I don't want to know Him."

Let me give you a word picture that may help you understand this a little clearer. I want you to imagine earth and all of life as a fifty-story high-rise. And since it will bring vivid memories, let's make it in downtown New York City.

In the basement and coming up through level 1 is an explosion. Fire and smoke are rising and it's heating up the building. Little by little it's moving up very slowly floor by floor.

Jesus arrives, and He is the ultimate fireman. He walks all fifty floors and knocks on every door. He tells everyone, "There's a fire coming and this building is going down. Follow me and I'll get you out of here."

One door opens into an office full of people. They tell Him that they will find their own way down and leave once their important business is done. Jesus tells them that the fire is coming up the right side of the building. There is only one way to escape, and they must exit through the narrow passage.

He knocks on another door and finds a couple. They are on their honeymoon and not interested in leaving. They don't smell smoke and tell Jesus to leave them alone. Jesus pleads with them to get out, but they don't listen and close the door on Him.

He goes to another floor and knocks on more doors. One man doesn't even listen to Jesus and continues focusing on his plan for the day.

Jesus goes from door to door, seeking to rescue people. And after the last person who really wants to leave the building gets out, the building is consumed in flames, and Jesus forfeits His life saving the last person.

The only people who remain in the building are there because they chose to be there. The only people who end up in hell are the people who don't want anything to do with God. They are people who demand to be in control of their own lives and only want their way.

As tears come down the face of the fireman's Father, Jesus steps back and lets them have their own way. Hell is the place to allow people to have the freedom to reject God if they want to. The Scripture is emphatic that God finds no joy in the death of the wicked, but His desire is that all would repent (change their mind about God and life) and be saved.

What if this is true? What if your neighbors and mine, your friends, the guy who you joke with at work, don't know about Christ? Does your heart and life act like there really is a heaven and a hell? Do you have a sense of urgency? I wonder how differently we would live if we really believed in a literal heaven and a literal hell. I wonder how much we are distracted by media, movies, life, games, stuff, sports, money, and dreams that really won't mean much one day.

> I wonder how differently we would live if we really believed in a literal heaven and a literal hell.

It's important to deeply ponder the hope and the reality of heaven and hell. Some of the people who are going to be in hell are some of the nicest people you've ever met and some of the most religious.

It's not going to be full of only axe murderers, wife beaters, child abusers, and other horrible people. You can be in absolute rebellion against God and clothe it with all kinds of religiosity and arrogance. The harshest words that ever came out of Jesus' mouth were to religious people filled with hypocrisy—the Pharisees.

Jesus tells us there is life after death. This life is not all about you, and it is not about me. It's not about sports, getting into the right school, or how your body looks. It's not about our little world of self-fulfillment. We are living in this one, singular point in time, but there is an eternity ahead of us, and we need to live in view of that eternity. So let me help you get really clear on what heaven and hell will be like.

A Preview of Heaven—the Great Adventure

God so loved the world that He gave His Son. He has made the greatest sacrifice so everyone who would turn to Him in faith can be with Him in heaven.

> For God so loved the world that he gave his one and only Son, that whoever believes in him shall not perish but have eternal life. For God did not send his Son into the world to condemn the world, but to save the world through him. (John 3:16–17)

God wants to be with you! That is the whole point of the Bible! The Bible tells us in Revelation 21:1–5,

> Then I saw "a new heaven and a new earth," for the first heaven and the first earth had passed away, and there was no longer any sea. I saw the Holy City, the new Jerusalem, coming down out of heaven from God, prepared as a bride beautifully dressed for her husband. And I heard a loud voice from the throne saying, "Look! God's dwelling place is now among the people, and he will dwell with them. They will be his people, and God himself will be with them and be their God. 'He will wipe every tear from their eyes. There will be no more death' or mourning or crying or pain, for the old order of things has passed away."
>
> He who was seated on the throne said, "I am making everything new!" Then he said, "Write this down, for these words are trustworthy and true."

Heaven is where God is, and it is characterized by beauty, light, and warmth (Rev. 4:1–4; 22:1–5). There are wonderful relationships (Heb. 12:22–24) and incredible accommodations (John 14:1–3). You get a fresh start (1 John 3:2) no matter where you have been, no matter what has happened to your body, no matter your past. You will receive a new nature, a new body, and a new vocation.

There is complete rest, protection, contentment, security, peace, and purpose. It's a place of unbridled joy, celebration, worship, laughter, and music (Matt. 26:29). Contrary to the idea that we will just be floating around on clouds in one long worship service, there will be fellowship, worship, serving, and eating. We will discover the infinite majesty of God and be present with Him forever (Rev. 5:8–9; Rev. 21–22).

The new earth will be familiar and similar to what we know in this life, but it will be infinitely better. Everything you have experienced in this life and everything you love about this earth is just a glimpse of what is to come. Think through your "best of" list . . . the new earth will be all of that and so much more.

The Bible gives us pictures and metaphors of heaven as a great banquet, a celebration, a party, a marriage, and a great family reunion. It's the most exciting adventure ever. People will be aligned in purpose, working together and doing the greatest thing in all the world in the perfect environment.

> Think through your "best of" list . . . the new earth will be all of that and so much more.

You'll have a new relationship with God and a new relationship with sin. Sin will be gone and, along with it, abuse, regrets, betrayal, divorce, failure, disappointments, rejection, prejudice, poverty, and injustice. God defeated it all.

C. S. Lewis says that in heaven you'll "become more human than you ever succeeded in being on earth."[5] You will finally be who you were meant to be, and that is what heaven will be like.

If you'd like to continue your learning about heaven, I invite you to read my book called *The Real Heaven: What the Bible Actually Says.*

A Preview of Hell—the Horrible Choice

What is hell like? Most importantly, God is not there. Second Thessalonians 1:9 says hell is absence from the presence of God. The Bible also describes punishment and torment (Rev.14:10–11) in varying degrees (Matt. 11:21–24) based on the knowledge that people had and their response to it.

Some of you have been through the pain of the loss of a child, others the pain of a divorce or clinical depression. If you have been through these kinds of losses, you know what it is like to feel that depth of darkness and loneliness. The darkness (Matt. 8:12), weeping, wailing, and gnashing of teeth (Matt. 13:40–42) are all included in hell. It is forever (Heb. 6:2; Rev. 14:11).

People often joke about going to hell. You may hear people joke that their life is already hell, so they might as well go there. Hell is not a joke, and it is not trivial. Hell is the absence of light, love, meaning, purpose, and God's presence.

The Reasons for a Hell

Hell is one of the most misunderstood concepts in all of Scripture. Because we have heard very little teaching on the subject,

most of us have heard hell depicted as a place of eternal torment where a callous and capricious God sends people who
disagree with Him. By contrast, the scriptural basis for hell
reveals that it is rooted in the dignity of man and the holiness
of God. Let's look at the real reasons there must be a hell.

Man's Dignity and Freedom Demand a Hell

God created man in His image and gave him the freedom
of choice. The freedom to love Him or freedom to refuse
Him. God is granting man dignity in giving him what he
has chosen.

C. S. Lewis says it this way:

> If a game is played, it must be possible to lose it. If the hap-
> piness of a creature lies in self-surrender, no one can make
> that surrender but himself (though many can help him make
> it) and he may refuse. I would pay any price to be able to say
> truthfully, "All will be saved." But my reason retorts "Without
> their will, or with it?" If I say "Without their will" I at once
> perceive a contradiction; how can the supreme, voluntary
> act of self-surrender be involuntary? And if I say "With their
> will," my reason replies "How if they *will not* give in?"[6]

C. S. Lewis described hell as a place where you are locked, but
the locks are on the inside. The people inside never wanted
anything to do with God, and they didn't want to be with
God. Will there be regret and remorse? Absolutely.

God's Holiness and Justice Demand a Hell

I want you to think of the three people whom you love the
most. They may be your children, your mate, or your best

friend. Have you got them pictured in your mind? Imagine all three of them are in a room when someone comes through the door with a gun.

Then *bam, bam, bam*. The three people you love so much are dead. The person who committed this horrible crime is caught, handcuffed, and arraigned. They bring the person in for the trial and before the judge. The judge asks, "What in the world did you do and why?" The response is, "You know, I had a really bad day. My coffee was cold, breakfast stunk, I had a bad day at work, and I got depressed. I was so mad that I killed people."

The judge turns as you're sitting there weeping and mourning over what you have lost and he announces, "Everybody has a bad day. Try not to do this again. Next case." How do you feel about that? You would be outraged, and the judge would be despicable in your eyes. Why? Because you are made in the image of God, and God is holy and just. As awful as the idea of hell is to us as human beings, it is more awful to consider a universe, a God, and an eternity that are not just and fair.

Sin's Seriousness Demands a Hell

We are living in a day when people don't take sin seriously. God made the world, and He made all of us for intimate relationship with Him. Sin, that first act of rebellion by our first parents, was passed on to each one of us. The word *sin* literally means to "miss the mark." It's the picture of an archer shooting for a target and the arrow falling short. Sin is the word that describes the human race's willful rebellion against our Creator. We have fallen short of His benevolent desires and are in rebellion against Him. Sin is like a cancer that entered the human race, bringing jealousy, envy, selfishness, wars, abuse, corruption, and ultimately death.

Sin was so serious that the only remedy for a holy God was for His Son to come and save us from it. God's love never changed for mankind; but man's sin has separated him from intimate relationship with a holy God. The only solution was drastic! God the Son would take on human flesh, being born of a virgin that He might be fully God and fully man. The theologians call it the *hypostatic union*—Jesus' nature is perfect humanity and undiminished deity without confusion. Being human He could die; being fully God, His death could be a substitute and atoning sacrifice for the sins of all humanity.

> Sin is like a cancer that entered the human race.

When Jesus died on the cross, His blood atoned or covered the sins of all people of all time, making everyone savable (1 John 2:1–2). At the cross the penalty of sin was paid for once and for all (Rom. 5), the power of sin was broken (Rom. 6), Satan was defeated (Col. 2), and death was swallowed up in victory (1 Cor. 15). God demonstrated the victory over sin, death, and Satan by the resurrection of Jesus and by the empowering work of the Holy Spirit in His followers. But make no mistake, the cost to resolve the problem of sin and make salvation available to "whoever believes in him [Jesus]" makes rejecting the free offer of God's saving grace the most serious of offenses with the most serious of consequences.

Evil's Defeat Demands a Hell

The final reason there must be a hell might take you by surprise. We tend to be so focused on the visible world that we forget there is an invisible world and a very significant history that occurred before mankind was even created. Evil is

Sin was so serious that the only remedy for a holy God was for His Son to come and save us from it.

introduced early in the biblical narrative. The source of this evil is a fallen angel named Lucifer or the devil. Isaiah 14 and Ezekiel 28 reveal that the source of his sin is pride and his attempt to usurp God's throne.

The Scripture teaches us that he led a rebellion against God and that a third of the angels of heaven joined him. Satan and these fallen angels, now called demons, have sought to overrule and destroy the work of God by attacking all that is good, deceiving the world, and thwarting God's purposes for His chosen people.

One of God's final judgments is to remove evil from His presence forever. To do so He created a place where evil will be encapsulated and removed forever from His presence and those He loves. Revelation 20:10 describes His final judgment on Satan and demons: "And the devil, who deceived them, was thrown into the lake of burning sulfur, where the beast and the false prophet had been thrown. They will be tormented day and night for ever and ever."

Conclusion

When I opened this chapter, I told you a story of a group of young people who claimed to believe that nothing exists after we die. Yet in the face of their close friend's death, they talked about "peace" and a "better place." It's one thing to argue philosophically, but it's something quite different to face the reality of death.

This is a hard chapter to swallow. Not because the evidence for life after death is weak, but because the implications are so emotionally overwhelming. It's hard to swallow because it goes so contrary to the squishy love that we have been hearing for the last few decades and the pluralism that says, "Everyone is okay no matter what they believe or how they live." We all know intuitively that is not true, but it's an unpopular and narrow road to travel.

> Everyone is going to die, everyone is going to live forever, and everyone will be judged.

Jesus is the only one who has come back from the dead, and He has proven by His resurrection that His teaching is true. So let me summarize what we've learned in the form of a question and a few final comments.

Will your eternal future be a blissful adventure or a horrible experience? We have said there are significant reasons to believe there is life after death. Everyone is going to die, everyone is going to live forever, and everyone will be judged.

> Think hard and deeply about the reality of heaven and hell.

For those of you who are followers of Christ, my plea would be this: Think hard and deeply about the reality of heaven and hell. We live in a "right-now" world that is filled with distractions. We rarely think deeply about eternity until someone we love dies. My prayer is that you will take stock of your life and relationships. If heaven and hell are real, is there someone God is prompting you to really pray for and talk to?

And for those of you who are not sure where you are going to spend your eternity, take time to really evaluate what you believe. Jesus has paid for your sin and given you a way to spend forever in heaven with God. Will you receive the gift He is offering you?

6

Why I Believe in Creation

The heavens declare the glory of God; the skies proclaim
the work of his hands.

Psalm 19:1

I grew up in a house of educators. My mother and father both
held advanced degrees beyond their bachelor's. My father
was a math and science teacher, and my mother was a high
school guidance counselor.

I didn't think much of it growing up, but life at the Ingram
household was one continual educational seminar. I remember my dad letting me go to school with him and the ex-
citement I had watching the science experiments. He would
explain the periodic table, pour things into test tubes that
would cause smoke through chemical reactions, and take
me out at night with his class to study the constellations in
the sky. He was an innovative teacher with a logical mind.

My mother, by contrast, was the most emotionally intelligent person I have ever met. Her concern for students going through the chaos of the '60s often meant troubled students staying at our house, and deep talks about life, situational ethics, and the perils of drugs. She was committed to helping us think for ourselves and make our own decisions based on what was right, what was wisest, and what would serve us and others in the long haul.

Every night we would eat dinner together and have discussions and even debates about science, psychology, values, and current events. I will be forever grateful for that early training in how to think, being open to new ideas, and the healthy skepticism concerning "what everyone says is right."

> Every night we would eat dinner together and have discussions and even debates about science, psychology, values, and current events.

We weren't an overly religious family, but we did attend church regularly. We believed in God but did not read the Bible, pray together, or have any knowledge of a personal relationship with God. My mother's spiritual roots were quite deep from her childhood and my father's were more of an outward form.

The result was a superficial faith that did not enter into our analysis or thinking of the world that we lived in, apart from obeying the Golden Rule, "Do to others what you would have them do to you" (Matt. 7:12). God was neatly compartmentalized in the values department with no thought of the implications in the arena of science. We weekly recited a creed about God creating and making everything and everyone, and at the same time unconsciously lived with a very empirical "scientific viewpoint" in everyday life.

I cannot remember one conversation about creation or evolution. We somehow allowed our minds to believe both simultaneously, with the sense that they each have their own worlds—one has to do with the metaphysical and it works for us, and the other has to do with the scientific and that works for us as well.

> These two worldviews in their purest forms are fundamentally in opposition to one another.

You can imagine the intellectual challenge it was for me when I was faced with the reality that these two worldviews in their purest forms are fundamentally in opposition to one another. So let me invite you on a journey to examine both creationism and Darwinian macroevolution. Let's begin by getting a lay of the land. Walk with me as we preview current debate.

The Origin of Life

The beauty, design, and complexity of our world has intrigued humanity for generations. Throughout human history and culture, creation stories abound. It seems hard to imagine that our world's entire existence happened by chance. Contemporary philosophers, theologians, and scientists have stated the argument like this:

1. The universe displays an incredible amount of order.
2. Either this order happened by chance or it is the result of some intelligent design.

3. Observation has never shown order happening by chance.
4. Therefore, it must be the product of intelligent design.
5. Since the design is the product of a designer, the universe is the product of a designer.

There are many critics of this argument who disagree with its premise. They suggest that the burden of proof is on the shoulders of those who believe in design to prove that it did not happen by chance. Perhaps order gradually developed by chance mutations over billions and billions of years.

The origins of life debate and what to teach our children has been argued in court for the last hundred years. In 1925 a substitute teacher named John Scopes was accused of violating Tennessee law when he taught students the theory of evolution in a public school. The case became very public. Coverage was available over the radio, and it was seen as a contest between religious beliefs and modern science.

The effects of that trial are still felt today. Nowadays, it is unlawful to present creationism or intelligent design in public education. In December 2005, in *Kitzmiller et al. v. Dover*, the district court judge ordered the Dover school board to not allow intelligent design principles (ideas that led to questioning gaps in Darwin's theory) to be taught in public schools. Intelligent design was seen as "religious" and not science.

Interestingly, public opinion keeps shifting, and in a recent popular opinion survey, Dr. John West discovered that

> Americans overwhelmingly agree that dissenting views in science are healthy:

- 84% of Americans believe that "attempts to censor or punish scientists for holding dissenting views on issues such as evolution or climate change are not appropriate in a free society."
- 94% of Americans believe "it is important for policy makers and the public to hear from scientists with differing views."
- 87% of Americans think that "people can disagree about what science says on a particular topic without being 'anti-science.'"
- 86% of Americans think that "disagreeing with the current majority view in science can be an important step in the development of new insights and discoveries."[1]

The Fundamental Question Is . . .

Is it intellectually feasible to believe that the God of the Bible created the world, the universe, and all living things? Or is classic atheistic evolution as taught in our schools a scientific fact that has empirically and logically been proven by means of the scientific method? Is life the product of a purely material universe that came into being by random chance or accident? The implications of this question are huge.

Before we begin our journey, let's take a look at the two primary theories on origins. There are variations of these two theories that we will address later.

Evolution

Evolution, specifically macroevolution, is the origin of life theory developed by Charles Darwin. It includes two main points: first, that everything in life is related through one common ancestor, and second, that diversity in species occurred through modifications by natural selection over long periods of time. Evolutionary theory teaches that the origin and development of life has been and is increasing from simple to complex over time. As modern science developed, Darwin's view of natural selection was not sufficient on its own, and the addition of transmission of genetic code from parent to offspring was added to the theory.

You may have heard of the term *microevolution*, which refers to the small changes that only happen within a species. Some examples of microevolution are the mosquito's ability to resist DDT after years of exposure, or the ability of different bacterial strains to resist penicillin. No scientist or theologian questions the validity of microevolution (modification within a species).

Darwin saw microevolution as evidence of macroevolution. From this point on, whenever I use the term *evolution*, I am referring to Darwin's theory of macroevolution—the vertical transition between species (from one kind of species to another kind) evolving to account for all animal and human life.

Creation

The theory of creation is the belief that God created all things out of nothing, as described in the Bible in the book of Genesis. All of life in its rich complexity happened as the result of the all-powerful, all-knowing, sovereign God of the universe who is maker of heaven and earth, of all things visible and invisible by the Word of His power.

> In the beginning God created the heavens and the
> earth. Now the earth was formless and empty,
> darkness was over the surface of the deep, and the
> Spirit of God was hovering over the waters.
> And God said, "Let there be light," and there was
> light. God saw that the light was good, and
> he separated the light from the darkness. God
> called the light "day," and the darkness he called
> "night." And there was evening, and there was
> morning—the first day. (Gen. 1:1–5)

The Son is the image of the invisible God, the firstborn over all creation. For in him all things were created: things in heaven and on earth, visible and invisible, whether thrones or powers or rulers or authorities; all things have been created through him and for him. He is before all things, and in him all things hold together. And he is the head of the body, the church; he is the beginning and the firstborn from among the dead, so that in everything he might have the supremacy. (Col. 1:15–18)

Exposing the Controversy

The creation versus evolution debate is a long one, spanning nearly one hundred years. However, in more recent times, the issues and the debate have become far more complex. At the risk of oversimplifying the issues, I want to give you a brief overview of the four major views in the current debate and share some direct quotes from the various proponents. Afterward, I will compare and contrast the two classic positions that represent creation by the God of the Bible and atheistic macroevolution by Darwin.

1. The Classic Macroevolution Position

This position presumes that a very simple form of life began by random chance. Then that simple living organism mutated and evolved over millions of years into all of the species today, including human life. The most notable proponents are Carl Sagan and Richard Dawkins, and this is the position held in universities and taught in public schools.

2. The New Voices Challenging the Macroevolution Position

A growing number of scientists have challenged some of the most basic tenets of evolution. These voices include Michael Behe, author of *Darwin's Black Box: The Biochemical Challenge to Evolution*; Michael Denton, author of *Evolution: A Theory in Crisis*; Francis Crick, Nobel laureate; and Søren Løvtrup, author of *Darwin: The Refutation of a Myth*. To be clear, these voices are not necessarily advocating creationism but are simply challenging macroevolution and its basic answers to origin and the development of life.

> A growing number of scientists have challenged some of the most basic tenets of evolution.

3. The Theistic Evolutionists

This group of scientists and theologians see God as the Creator who has used the evolutionary process to accomplish His magnificent work. They unapologetically take God, the Bible, and evolution very seriously. Notable proponents include Dennis Alexander, author of *Creation or Evolution: Do We Have to Choose?*; Keith Miller, author of *Perspectives on an Evolving*

Creation; and Francis Collins, author of *The Language of God: A Scientist Presents Evidence for Belief*. Collins is also known for his discovery of disease genes and for his leadership of the Human Genome Project. All three scientists are Christians.

4. Intelligent Design

Intelligent design is the view that the complexity of life is best explained by an intelligent cause, not an undirected cause like natural selection. This group of scientists encompasses creationists, theistic evolutionists, and agnostics. What they all share in common is their opposition to the primary premise of mainstream evolution—that life began by random chance. They instead believe the most recent scientific discoveries argue for some intelligence. They may disagree on the source and nature of that intelligence, but they all challenge classical Darwinian evolution.

What I want you to understand is that the creation versus evolution debate has taken some major turns in the last few decades. Some scientists who don't necessarily believe in God are major critics of classic Darwinian evolution. Nearly as surprising are Christians who do not see a contradiction between evolution and Christian teaching on creation from the Bible.

Perhaps the following table will help you visualize the current state of the debate.

The Origin and Development of Life

Option 1	Option 2	Option 3	Option 4
Classic Creationism	Theistic Evolution	Intelligent Design	Classic Evolution
(The literal biblical account)	(God-supervised evolution)	(A designer of some kind)	(Random chance and natural selection)

Historically, there are two main options—classic creationism and classic Darwinian evolution. Although it is important to know the distinctions within these two broad views, the man on the street and/or the student in the classroom is taught evolution as a fact and creationism as an anti-intellectual, nonscientific, religious crutch.

Now that we have surveyed the various views on life's origins, let's take a few moments to hear from a variety of experts who support various positions. I think you'll be surprised by some of the current debates and thinking by Christians and non-Christians alike.

One biblical creationist writes,

> The field of science is our human attempt to observe, understand, and explain what we see in the world around us. Scientific theory is observable, testable and repeatable. I want you to take a moment to imagine what it may have been like to witness the beginning of life and of the universe. The challenge remains that no one witnessed the moment of creation or the moment one organism evolved into another. We only see small changes, not large ones, and the changes don't increase in complexity. It is important for us to understand that all the theories on origin are based on circumstantial evidence.[2]

By contrast, evolution is taught as scientific fact, and scientists see its acceptance as part of their training. We have been taught in public schools and universities that it is the only option unless you are narrow-minded, anti-intellectual, and nonscientific. In other words, evolution is a proven fact. There's science and intellect, then there are people who need supernatural, religious crutches to explain life.

If that sounds a bit strong, read the following four quotes that capture the mainstream view of evolution.

Our theory of evolution has become . . . one which cannot be refuted by any possible observation. Every conceivable observation can be fitted into it. It is thus "outside of empirical science" but not necessarily false. No one can think of ways in which to test it. Ideas either without basis or based on a few laboratory experiments carried out in extremely simplified systems have attained currency far beyond their validity. They have become part of an evolutionary dogma accepted by most of us as part of our training.[3]

One of the most famous and strongest spokesmen for evolution was Cornell University professor Carl Sagan. His book *Cosmos* remains one of the bestselling science books of all time. It was on the *New York Times* Bestseller list for seventy weeks. Sagan flat out states that evolution is a fact, not a theory.[4]

The renowned scientist Richard Dawkins has been another strong voice for evolution, and he says, "The theory of evolution by cumulative natural selection is the only theory we know of that is in principle capable of explaining the existence of organized complexity. Even if the evidence did not favour it, it would still be the best theory available!"[5]

Bill Nye, the science guy, is a favorite scientist and educator to students throughout the country. His award-winning PBS shows, TV appearances, videos, and books have increased his popularity. In one of his videos, he uses emojis to explain the theory of evolution. Evolution is "undeniable" and creationism "inane," according to Nye.[6]

In recent years, however, classic evolution has been challenged as a result of scientific discoveries that undermine some of its most basic presuppositions.

Complexity of Life

The crux of the argument for both evolution and creation seems to rest on the idea of complexity of life. Evolution views the complexity of life as a result of billions of years of adaption and living things moving from simple to complex in order to survive. Creation views the complexity of life as evidence of an all-knowing Creator.

In 1984, three scientists named Charles B. Thaxton, Walter L. Bradley, and Roger L. Olsen, with doctorates in chemistry, material science, and geochemistry respectively, wrote *The Mystery of Life's Origin*, the first comprehensive critique of chemical evolution. The results of their mathematical equations and chemical formulas raised serious questions about the feasibility of life starting through chemical reactions.

Dean Kenyon of San Francisco State University said the book was full of fresh ideas and original critiques of chemical evolution. He was puzzled that other scientists had not voiced similar criticism of chemical evolution. According to Kenyon, many scientists hesitate to admit that there could be problems within chemical evolution because it would open the door to the possibility of a supernatural origin of life.

It wasn't that long ago Darwinian scientists would have never considered the validity of any book criticizing chemical evolution and advocating creation. Yet, the *Yale Journal of*

Biology and Medicine gave *The Mystery of Life's Origin* high marks:

> The volume as a whole is devastating to a relaxed acceptance of current theories of abiogenesis. It is well written, and, though technical, much of the book is within the reach of the informed non-scientist. The book apparently has been well received by many who are working in the field of abiogenesis, such as Dean Kenyon and Robert Shapiro. . . . This book is . . . strongly recommended to anyone interested in the problem of chemical and biological origins.[7]

Scientists are looking at the facts and allowing what they find to change their worldview. Many are beginning to see a theory that's been biased for years. The more scientists learned about DNA and the amazing intricacy inside a human cell, the more questions challenging evolution began to surface. Biochemist and agnostic Michael Denton said in his book *Evolution: A Theory in Crisis* that evolution's intellectual foundations have been steadily eroding. Biology's new findings are bringing us very near to a formal, logical disproval of Darwinian claims. Denton believes Darwin's claim that all life evolved from one cell can't be supported by evidence found in fossils, embryology, taxonomy, and molecular biology.[8]

Nobel laureate Francis Crick proposed that the problems of life randomly originating on earth are so great that life must have arisen elsewhere in the universe and been transported here. Crick admits that his commitment to materialism and his hostility toward religion motivated him to enter his field of science. "I went into science because of religious reasons. There's no doubt about it. I asked myself, what were the things that appear inexplicable and are used to support religious beliefs?" Then Crick sought to show that those things have a purely material foundation. His feelings toward religion led him to find scientific evidence to undermine religious belief. Fellow scientist Steven Weinberg confessed his hope that science would liberate people from religion and it became a motivating force in his life.[9]

Can you imagine the courage it takes in today's scientific community to support scientific research that doesn't agree with Darwinian macroevolution? Those who take this stand may find it hard to be tenured in their universities or published in scientific journals, and yet this group of scientists is growing.

Swedish embryologist Søren Løvtrup, in his book *Darwinism: The Refutation of a Myth*, wrote, "I believe that one day, the Darwinian myth will be ranked as the greatest deception in the history of science and when this happens, many people will pose the question, how did this ever happen?"[10]

I think it is important, as we examine this topic, that you are aware of some of the dissenting voices in the scientific community.

We need to be thinking Christians. The Bible commands us to love the Lord our God with all our heart, with all our soul, and with all our MIND (Luke 10:27). We need to learn how to think and follow God with our minds. Darwinian evolution is a faith construct, not a scientific fact.

People like to think they are objective, but no one is purely objective. We all have presuppositions. As followers of Christ, we have presuppositions that lead us to believe certain truths by faith and look at evidence through a particular lens.

Others may have a presupposition that came from a lack of faith, or out of woundedness or bad experiences with God, church, and Christians. All of us view scientific data through our presuppositional lenses.

It is hard to admit that we have a bias and that we are all defensive to some degree. We want to defend what we've been taught; but let's look at the two classic origin theories together and ask ourselves what we passionately believe to be true. What do the facts say? What presuppositions do I have? Am I willing to look at all the positions? As you read through the following series of questions, I encourage you to evaluate where you stand on creation and historic Darwinian evolution and why.

> All of us view scientific data through our presuppositional lenses.

Question 1: How did life begin?

Option #1: Evolution as taught in mainstream America

According to the Association of Biology Teachers, evolution's answer is that life's beginning was an unsupervised, impersonal, unpredictable natural process. The beginning of life was random and undirected, without either plan or purpose.[11]

Option #2: Creation as taught from a historical, literal, grammatical, biblical perspective

In contrast, creation's answer is that in the beginning, God created the heavens and the earth (Gen. 1:1).

You have two options when you look at all of life's order, design, and beauty. One, that everything we see was the result of random chance and random material over billions of years. There was no design, no purpose, and no intelligence that caused that single cell to burst forth into life. It takes faith to believe that all of life's order was birthed out of a random moment, and faith to assume how the raw material came to be.

It also takes faith to believe in the second option, that in the beginning God spoke and He created. It takes faith to believe what we read in Scripture, namely that the harmony, beauty, and complexity of the universe is a reflection of the character of an all-knowing, all-powerful Creator God.

> You alone are the Lord. You made the heavens, even the highest heavens, and all their starry host, the earth and all that is on it, the seas and all that is in them. You give life to everything, and the multitudes of heaven worship you. (Neh. 9:6)

Question 2: Why did life begin?

Option #1: Classic evolution

Evolution's response is that life began as a pure accident. It was random chance. Our solar system, our universe, and our little planet Earth exist because everything needed for life to begin just happened to be present in that exact moment. There was no design, no plan, no meaning, no emotions, no purpose, and no value.

Many evolutionary psychologists tell us that what we thought were feelings of love, pain, sorrow, joy, and purpose in life are nothing more than chemical reactions inside our brain developed over billions of years. These chemical reactions have allowed us to rise to the top of the animal species and are the main reason we have survived.

Feelings are only illusions and part of biochemical programming. The feelings that bring you a sense of meaning and purpose in your life are simply reactions to chemicals in your brain. Those feelings of love when you hold a newborn baby or the sense that you are part of something bigger when you see a sunset are merely the evolutionary development of mankind.

If we're logically consistent with this thinking, then life is a biochemical process, the result of pure accidental and random chance, and I am not accountable for any of my choices. My feelings and decisions are the result of chemical reactions that were pre-wired in my brain. Biologist William Provine has reputedly stated, "Evolution is the greatest engine of atheism." You see, once you get rid of a creator, all moral law falls apart. All sense of accountability is illogical and all rules are gone. Biologist Thomas Huxley claimed that Darwin gave us an excuse to live the way we really want to.

Option #2: Creation

In the Christian view, by contrast, you are the special creation of a good and all-powerful God. You are the climax of His creation. Not only is your kind unique but you are unique among your kind. Your Creator loves you so much and so intensely that He desires your companionship and affection, that He gave the life of His only Son that you might spend eternity with Him.

Scripture teaches that God made man in His own image to share fellowship with Him, to glorify Him, and to steward the earth.

> So God created mankind in his own image,
>   in the image of God he created them;
>   male and female he created them.
>
> God blessed them and said to them, "Be fruitful and increase in number; fill the earth and subdue it. Rule over the fish in the sea and the birds in the sky and over every living creature that moves on the ground" (Gen. 1:27–28).

There is an innate sense among all cultures that we are not simply at the top of the evolutionary chain, but that life has inherent meaning and purpose. Art, music, poetry, and creativity for its own sake argue against a purely material explanation of the human species. We are unique and different from all other creatures. We're made in the image of God, and being in the image of God, we can think, we can choose, and we have self-awareness, a conscience, and feelings of joy, sadness, delight, and love. We have purpose and meaning in life. Our physical life has a beginning and an end.

Life and eternity, according to Ecclesiastes 3:11, have been set in our hearts: "He has made everything beautiful in its time. He has also set eternity in the human heart; yet no one can fathom what God has done from beginning to end."

Human beings have a built-in moral awareness. It is that sense of "ought" and of "should" that all people have in common that C. S. Lewis addresses in *Mere Christianity*. It was this sense of right and wrong that led Lewis, an intellectual agnostic, to trust in Christ. Where did the sense of right and wrong come from?

Intellectual integrity demands that we all have to make a decision. How did life begin? Evolution or creation? Why did life begin? Was life an accident, a random chance, or could God have created us to enjoy fellowship with Him?

> There is an innate sense among all cultures that we are not simply at the top of the evolutionary chain, but that life has inherent meaning and purpose.

It is intellectually dishonest to put God in the "values compartment" like I did growing up and not deal with all the facts. I was intellectually bipolar. When it came to relationships, purpose, values, and meaning, my family and I believed that there was a God who provided hope, love, and heaven when you die.

But in my studies and worldview, I accepted evolution like every other eighth grader. I didn't know the transitional pictures in the textbook of ape to man were just models and conjecture, and I certainly didn't want to be seen as anti-intellectual or a religious fanatic. Yet this salad-bar approach of picking and choosing what "truth" I wanted to accept out of various options was really a cop-out.

Conclusion

So, how about you? What do you really believe and why? Who are you afraid of disappointing? How fearless are you willing to be to examine all sides of this critical issue and decide for yourself?

God does not want you to throw your brains in the trash to follow Him. In fact, why not grab a cup of coffee or tea and take a moment right now to really ponder where you stand? Then read the next chapter with me as we dig into the fossil record, the most recent biological discoveries, genetics, the Big Bang Theory, and the moral and sociological implications of creation and evolution.

7

Science or God

The False Dichotomy

He was young and smart. In fact, he was a Stanford grad student with a mind like a razor blade but a heart that was searching. I met him in my home as he was invited to gather with a number of young professionals in the Silicon Valley to explore "Love, Sex, and Lasting Relationships." The room was packed with those in their twenties and early thirties.

Externally it looked like the United Nations, as Asian, Indian, Hispanic, African-American, Arab, Anglo, and Armenian young professionals learned what the Bible said about relationships. Then they broke into six or seven groups around my house to discuss the implications of what they learned for their high-stress, high-tech, highly educated worlds where time and meaningful relationships were in short supply.

After the groups finished, people milled around for about an hour, eating snacks and getting to know one another. As I leaned against the counter in search of a second round of cheese and crackers, this young man struck up a conversation. He thanked me for opening our home and then made it very clear that despite the warm reception of the group, he had no room for God in his life because he was a scientist.

He then flatly stated that God and science are incompatible. Science is factual, empirical, observable, and based on what we can see and test. He went on to inform me that since God cannot be proven, observed, or tested, he simply had to eliminate that worldview as a possibility.

That statement started a long and interesting conversation. Ironically, his scientific worldview was not providing much help in his quest for love and meaningful relationships. He appreciated the people, the community, and a sense of belonging and authenticity that he observed, but in essence he said, "I can't throw my brains in the trash simply because I'm having a good experience or have emotional needs."

> Macro Darwinism as well as creationism are rooted in faith assumptions.

This wasn't the first time I had heard this comment and I'm sure it won't be the last. His bias and presuppositions kept him from even honestly exploring the biggest issues of his life—meaning, purpose, love, origins, and reality.

In this chapter, I would like to break down that false dichotomy of science or God and look at the issues and the facts. Macro Darwinism as well as creationism are rooted in faith assumptions. We all live by faith. No one observed the creation of the world and therefore it can never be scientifically verified. But there is a big difference between faith and "blind faith."

> Explore the facts and suspend the presuppositions on which you've built your faith.

I invite you now to explore the facts and to suspend the presuppositions (at least temporarily) on which you've built your faith. Let's look together at some of the fundamental questions of life and science that evolution and creation seek to explain.

Question 3: How did various plants and animals develop?

According to classic evolution, a simple cell slowly evolved into more complex plants and animals through the process of time, chance, natural selection, mutations, and survival of the fittest.

Before and after *The Origin of Species*, people believed in spontaneous generation. In 1860, a year after Darwin wrote his famous book, Louis Pasteur proved to the world that spontaneous generation was not possible. Life cannot come from non-life. An animal cannot come from an inanimate object.

On our planet, over six hundred million different species exist. Evolution's "faith statement" says that all species came from one simple, single cell. In contrast, creation's "faith statement" says that God created the extensive variety of life.

The Scriptures state emphatically,

> For since the creation of the world God's invisible qualities—
> his eternal power and divine nature—have been clearly seen,
> being understood from what has been made so that people
> are without excuse. (Rom. 1:20)

God created various plants, animals, and species in a harmonic balance to reflect His attributes and character. When you look into the stars, the consistency and orderliness of the galaxies provide evidence of His existence. God created balance and beauty. Our planet is perfectly held in rotation between the gravitational pull of the sun and Jupiter. Jupiter's size with its strong gravity attracts large rocks and keeps them from striking earth. The size of our moon keeps our planet in perfect tilt. The earth occupies a rare and unique place in all the universe where life can actually happen.

God did all of this so we would know He is the God of wisdom, intelligence, beauty, harmony, and eternity.

Long before people had telescopes, the inspiration of the Holy Spirit led the psalmist to write,

> The heavens declare the glory of God;
>   the skies proclaim the work of his hands.
> Day after day they pour forth speech;
>   night after night they reveal knowledge.
> They have no speech, they use no words;
>   no sound is heard from them.
> Yet their voice goes out into all the earth,
>   their words to the ends of the world. (Ps. 19:1–4)

Our world is an absolutely amazing place. Is this complex planet with beauty, balance, variety, and ecosystems a result of random chance, or does the evidence point to a grand design and therefore a Designer?

Question 4: Which theory best explains our most recent scientific discoveries?

I honestly think Darwinian evolution was a lot easier to believe prior to scientific advances in the late twentieth century. However, as technology has given us new insight into what was formerly invisible, Darwin's own words refute his theory:

> If it could be demonstrated that any complex organ existed, which could not possibly have been formed by numerous, successive, slight modifications, my theory would absolutely break down.[1]

When Darwin wrote *The Origin of Species* in 1859 and he looked at a cell through his microscope, he could not see what we are able to see today. Darwin, after all, had access to a microscope that would multiply only two to three hundred times. The cell seemed so uncomplicated when he looked at it through his microscope. In fact, Darwin himself used the word "simple" to describe single-cell organisms.

Molecular Biology

All Darwin saw when he looked through the microscope was a roundish mass surrounded by a membrane with a semi-liquid fluid. I remember reading in my school textbooks and seeing statements that declared the inside of the nucleus held nothing but clear fluid. Thanks to today's more powerful microscopes, we know that a single-cell organism, the most basic unit of any living thing, is incredibly complex.

In fact, it's so complicated that the greatest computers can't fully understand it, and creating cellular models has been a very challenging task. Some cells are so small that you need to use an electron microscope just to see them. They are small . . . very small. Small enough to fit 150,000 cells on the tip of a strand of hair.

Today molecular scientists describe a single cell as a high-tech factory. They are complete with artificial languages and decoding systems. They have central memory banks that store and retrieve impressive amounts of information. They have precise control systems that regulate the automatic assembly of the components and proofreading, quality-control mechanisms that safeguard against errors. They have assembly systems that use principles of prefabrication and modular construction. Can you imagine that all happening inside one little cell?

Cells also have a complete replication system that allows the organism to duplicate itself with bewildering speed. Charles Darwin was clearly wrong. A living cell, far from being simple, is one of the most amazing and complex things on the earth.

As I studied the scientific evidence of how a cell actually functions, it poked huge holes in my passive acceptance of the evolution I was taught in school.

Consider a simple illustration of the Law of Chance, provided by Abraham Cressy Morrison, chemist and president of the New York Academy of Sciences, in his book *Man Does Not Stand Alone*:

Suppose you take ten pennies and mark them from 1 to 10. Put them in your pocket and give them a good shake. Now try to draw them out in sequence from 1 to 10, putting each coin back in your pocket after each draw.

Your chance of drawing No. 1 is 1 to 10. Your chance of drawing 1 and 2 in succession is 1 in 100. Your chance of drawing 1, 2 and 3 in succession would be one in a thousand. Your chance of drawing 1, 2, 3 and 4 in succession would be one in 10,000 and so on, until your chance of drawing from No. 1 to No. 10 in succession would reach the unbelievable figure of one chance in 10 billion. The object in dealing with so simple a problem is to show how enormously figures multiply against chance.[2]

Now let's look at what must happen in one single cell for life to be viable.

A simple cell would need a vast number of parts. At least two hundred and thirty-nine protein molecules each containing four hundred and forty-five amino acids, all of which are made up of ten to twenty atoms. Of the hundreds of amino acids, only twenty are used in proteins. And they can't simply float around randomly.

In order for a protein to function, all four hundred and forty-five of them must be lined up in a single line in perfect, sequential order. For a single cell to spring to life, four hundred and forty-five amino acids would have to accidentally line up perfectly. Not once, but two hundred and thirty-nine times to form twenty-nine proteins to make a living cell.[3]

What I quoted here is what science has observed. These are facts of how life and a single cell actually look. This is why a number of non-Christian scientists today look at the evidence and say this can't happen by chance, no matter how many billions of years are added to the equation.

Genetics

The complexity of the cell is amazing, but let's dig even deeper. We know that DNA is contained within every cell. DNA is like the software of the cell, the computer program that makes it work. In fact, if you took a teaspoon and filled it to the top with this DNA, your teaspoon could contain the precise instructions to build every single species of organism that has ever existed on the planet, estimated at six hundred to one thousand million species. That is a lot of information in this one little teaspoon.

When you were still the size of a dot in your mother's womb, if it were possible to go in and remove your DNA and uncoil it, it would have been six feet tall. Your DNA would have encoded on it precise instructions for piecing together every part of your body. From your six hundred muscles to your two million optic nerves, to your one hundred billion nerve cells. Isn't that awesome? In fact, if the genetic information and DNA in a microscopic single-cell organism was spelled out in English, it would equal the whole volume of the *Encyclopaedia Britannica*.

Today's technological advances allow us to store incredible amounts of information. I am going to date myself, but I remember in college using microfiche. We thought it was really cool, and oh boy, can you imagine all this information on this little thing? Now I've got five thousand songs on my iPod, or I can stream almost any song I want to listen to. Compared to the DNA that God put in our bodies and every living thing, that is miniscule.

World-class expert in the chemistry of DNA Robert Shapiro was asked what he thought the chances were that DNA could have been formed by a random process. His answer: "None. It's absolute nonsense." Dr. Francis Crick, who shared the Nobel Prize for discovering DNA, said that he is convinced that life could not have ever evolved from non-living matter on the earth. This observation is not from a creationist or a Christian, but an atheist scientist looking objectively at the data.[4]

If we're going to be objective and really look at the data, the research, and the evidence, we'll find that the genius and the complexity of a single cell and DNA challenge the very core presuppositions of classic evolutionary thought.

In fact, the evolution of DNA is unbelievable. It is not its mere existence, but its staggering complexity. It's the divine computer program demonstrating that there must have been a Programmer.

Now let's turn our attention from that which is amazingly small to evidence in the skies above.

In Astronomy and Physics—the Big Bang

Albert Einstein published his equations of general relativity in 1915, and a Dutch astronomer named Willem de Sitter discovered a solution to them that predicted an expanding universe. The importance of these discoveries showed the world that the universe was expanding. If the galaxies were moving farther and farther apart, the implication was that they were once closer together. If the universe was expanding, then it must have had a starting point.

In 1923, Edwin Hubble observed the distant Andromeda nebula and calculated that it must be at least ten times farther away than the stars of the Milky Way. He predicted the galaxies were moving rapidly away from one another and that the universe was much larger than anyone had thought.

From this realization, Hubble went one step further. If galaxies that were twice as far away were moving away from each other at twice the speed, he reasoned, they must have begun their cosmic expansion from the same space at the same time. Using his distance/speed ratio, Hubble fixed that time at about two billion years ago. He was off by some ten to thirteen billion years by today's estimates, but he laid the foundation for the Big Bang Theory, providing evidence that the universe exploded into existence with a furious burst of energy and has been expanding ever since. It was a shattering blow to the centuries-old notion of a static universe.[5]

The theory of the expanding universe was consistent with Einstein's theory. Even so, the Big Bang, though thoroughly accepted in our day, was not originally accepted well by scientists.

Robert Jastrow, an American astronomer and planetary physicist, argues that the reason scientists were troubled by the notion of a Big Bang was because if it were true, it would imply that there was a moment of creation in which everything—the universe and its laws—came into existence.

He said in an interview with *Christianity Today*,

> Astronomers now find they have painted themselves into a corner because they have proven, by their own methods, that the world began abruptly in an act of creation to which you can trace the seeds of every star, every planet, every living thing in this cosmos and on the earth. And they have found that all this happened as a product of forces they cannot hope to discover. That there are what I or anyone would call supernatural forces at work is now, I think, a scientifically proven fact.[6]

In *God and the Astronomers*, Jastrow said, "For the scientist who has lived by his faith in the power of reason, the story ends like a bad dream. He has scaled the mountains of ignorance, he is about to conquer the highest peak; as he pulls himself over the final rock, he is greeted by a band of theologians who have been sitting there for centuries."[7]

> The Big Bang does not disprove classic evolution, but it argues strongly for a specific moment of creation.

Lest we allow some form of circular reasoning, it is very important to recognize that before the Big Bang, there were no laws of physics. In fact, the laws of physics cannot be used to explain the Big Bang because the Big Bang itself produced the laws of physics. To be fair, the Big Bang does not disprove classic evolution, but it argues strongly for a specific moment of creation.

Pause with me for just a moment. These are not the words and observations of pastors and theologians; they are the words of top scientists. I'm not throwing my brains in the trash or being anti-intellectual to question evolution. The facts of today's most recent scientific discoveries demand it.

Question 5: Which theory best explains the fossil record?

Darwin understood that there should be evidence of his origins theory of life within the fossil record. As you move backward in time in the geologic strata, one would expect to see a record of progressive life-forms. The early fossils would show a progressive transition from simple life-forms to more complex animal forms over billions and billions of years.

Darwin's Admission and Confidence of Future Discoveries

Why are there not progressive life-forms or intermediate links throughout geological formations and strata? According to Darwin, "The explanation lies, as I believe, in the extreme imperfection of the geological record."[8] Darwin thought such transitional species existed, but were not yet discovered. He believed he was on the front end of the journey and that scientists over time would uncover fossils that prove transitional life existed. So, let's examine Darwin's hypothesis and test it with the latest discoveries.

Present State of Fossil Records

Paleontology is the scientific study of life that existed in prior times and includes the study of fossils to determine organisms' evolution and interaction with each other and their environment. In their study of the strata of the earth called

150

the Cambrian Period, estimated around 542 million years ago, scientists observed a unique phenomenon that challenges Darwin's hypothesis. What we do find has been called the Cambrian Explosion; it's the appearance of rich biological diversity within an instant of geological time. Virtually a fossil blueprint of every animal phyla is evident in one stratum. This directly contradicts Darwin's theory of slow, gradual change.

I've taught on this before, and people email me with websites to visit and pictures of what they believe to be actual transitional life-forms. Most of them are artistic renderings based on scientific research. Dr. Colin Patterson, a senior paleontologist for the British Museum of Natural History, wrote a book for the British Museum simply called *Evolution*. Creationist and author Luther Sunderland wrote to Dr. Patterson asking why he had not shown a single photograph of a transitional fossil in his book. Patterson responded with this:

> I fully agree with your comments on the lack of direct illustration of evolutionary transitions in my book. If I knew of any, fossil or living, I would certainly have included them. You suggest that an artist should be used to visualize such transformations, but where would he get the information from? I could not, honestly, provide it, and if I were to leave it to artistic license, would that not mislead the reader?[9]

The lack of transitional forms in the fossil record is perhaps the most obvious and serious objection to Darwin's theory. We are now more than one hundred and fifty years after Darwin, and the knowledge of the fossil record has been greatly expanded. We have a quarter of a million fossil species, but the situation hasn't changed much. We have even fewer examples of evolutionary transition than we had in Darwin's time, and even Richard Dawkins admits in his book *The Blind Watchmaker* that there are significant gaps in the fossil record.

I hope you're beginning to see why I believe in creation. It is a faith proposition to be sure, but as I review this scientific evidence, it not only challenges the basic tenets of macro-evolution, it argues for intelligence, design, and complexity that demands a Creator.

I want to shift our thinking now from physical science to the social sciences. Darwinism and creationism have both had a significant impact on how we live and treat one another.

Question 6: Which theory or claim has the greatest moral or social benefit to mankind?

Darwinism and Humanism: God Dethroned

If something is true and positive, you would expect it to have a positive, fruitful impact on our relationships and life. So let's look at the moral and social benefits of Darwinism. Before the latter part of the nineteenth century when humanism was gaining traction, Darwinian evolution became the intellectual fodder for Nietzsche, Huxley, and later Hegel and others who did not believe God exists. In Darwinism and humanism, man becomes the center of the universe and God is dethroned. Huxley has been quoted as claiming that Darwin's theory has freed us and made it intellectually acceptable to be an atheist. There are no moral constraints. Instead of God, His law, and morality saying what is right or wrong, man gets to choose.

Dr. Thomas Nagel, a professor of philosophy and law at New York University, said it this way:

I speak from experience, being strongly subject to this fear myself: I want atheism to be true and am made uneasy by the fact that some of the most intelligent and well-informed people I know are religious believers. It isn't just that I don't believe in God and, naturally, hope that I'm right in my belief. It's that I hope there is no God! I don't want there to be a God; I don't want the universe to be like that. My guess is that this cosmic authority problem is not a rare condition and that it is responsible for much of the scientism and reductionism of our time. One of the tendencies it supports is the ludicrous overuse of evolutionary biology to explain everything about human life, including everything about the human mind. . . . This is a somewhat ridiculous situatio. . . . [I]t is just as irrational to be influenced in one's beliefs by the hope that God does not exist as by the hope that God does exist.[10]

Darwinism and Morality—Relative Truth Birthed

If there is no God, and no moral law, then man decides what is good, what is right, and what is wrong. Man decides who has value and who doesn't have value. What should we do? What should we not do? This philosophy of life is called humanism, and it grew out of the Enlightenment, which arose in the eighteenth century. During this period, people began to believe that man's reason, not God's revelation, was our primary authority. Darwin's later writings bolstered this notion and gave a sense of scientific justification and a worldview that was applied to social relationships. From there, relative truth was birthed and moral absolutes were progressively discarded.

As I was growing up, one of the most memorable practices of our family was that when we finished with dinner, everyone pushed their plates to the middle of the table, got a cup of coffee, and the nightly Ingram discussion would begin. (Note: It's probably why coffee became my "let's have a talk" drink of choice.)

We didn't have those "how was your day in school" discussions, followed by silence. That wouldn't fly in my house. For thirty, sometimes forty-five minutes we would tackle hot topics together. I still remember my mom coming home and talking about situational ethics. Like I said before, my parents were both educators and were deeply concerned that we would learn to think critically. As a guidance counselor, my mom saw the social implications of situational ethics played out in the free love and drug culture of the '60s and '70s.

The general population for centuries held to a moral law rooted in the belief of a moral lawgiver. The five-thousand-year-old prohibitions against murder, lying, stealing, adultery, and so forth, were accepted as absolutes. Evolution gave an intellectual basis for casting off the Creator (lawgiver) and thus any moral absolutes.

Intellectuals began to say, there is no creator God, so who's to determine what is true? We will decide what is right and what is wrong in various situations. Situational ethics was the tip of the iceberg of an existential philosophy that led to the sexual revolution and the explosion of thought to throw off all restraints. We heard phrases like, "I'm okay, you're okay" and "If it feels good, do it." The fruit of this worldview began to show itself in the disintegration of the family, heightened violence, and rampant spread of sexually transmitted diseases.

These are the results of a life guided by random chance, with no purpose, no designer, and no God. If you're just a blob on this little part of the solar system on this little planet, then it is intellectually consistent to say, like existentialist John Paul Sartre, "There is no meaning to life." If there is no meaning or purpose in life, then it is up to you to experience moments and create your own meaning. Who's to tell anyone what to do?

In the following decades, existentialism bloomed into the pluralism of our day that rejects any notion of Absolute Truth or moral standard. All truth claims have equal footing. Tolerance as defined by "no one can say what's right or wrong" has become the new mantra. Unfortunately, the casting off of moral restraint and the removal of a Creator has significant implications for relationships, meaning and purpose, and society in general.

> The casting off of moral restraint and the removal of a Creator has significant implications.

Darwinism and Racism, Sexism, Abortion

Let's examine the consistent application of classic Darwinian macroevolutionary thinking to social relationships. If life truly is survival of the fittest, we should keep the best. We should look at men and women and decide who is more important and more valuable and act accordingly. If we can make the world better by ethnic cleansing and getting rid of whole races that don't live up to our standard, do it. We, "the fittest" in Darwin's world, get to say who should live and who should die. This is the very worldview that fueled eugenics prior to World War II and the basis for the Nazi's attempt to eradicate the "lesser" races.

What are the logical applications of this worldview? Classic evolution justifies racism. Let me share with you Darwin's own perspective on race that might shock you. "The more civilised, so-called Caucasian races have beaten the Turkish hollow in the struggle for existence. Looking to the world at no very distant date, what an endless number of lower races will have been eliminated by the higher civilised races throughout the world."[11]

Building on Darwin's thinking, Huxley, a big fan of Darwin, wrote, "No rational man, cognizant of facts, believes that the average negro is equal, still less, the superior of the white man. It is simply incredible to think that he will be able to compete successfully with his bigger brained and smaller jawed rival in a contest which is to be carried on by thoughts and not by bites."[12] Sadly, this distorted worldview even infiltrated the church. Many Southern Christians prior to the Civil War held this same position and this misapplication of "survival of the fittest" has promoted views of racial superiority even to this day.

Darwin also said, "The chief distinction in the intellectual powers of the two sexes is shown by a man attaining to a higher eminence, in whatever he takes up, than woman can attain—whether requiring deep thought, reason, or imagination or merely the use of the senses and the hands, we may also infer that the average mental power in man must be above that of a woman."[13]

How many adamant Darwinian macroevolutionists want to step into Darwin's racism and gender bias and say it is the logical conclusion of survival of the fittest? Evolution has been used to justify racism, sexism, Nazism, and other hateful behavior. Please do not hear me say that Charles Darwin is personally at fault for all of this. But his "theory" provided the intellectual basis for some of the most hideous actions in world history. We're talking about people taking bits and pieces of Darwinian thought to support their evil actions.

Make no mistake, your worldview affects how you live. If you believe life began without a creator, that there is no designer, no God, and no truth, then the consistent application includes a survival of the fittest mentality with all of its implications. I am not saying that evolutionary thought caused these tragedies; I'm saying it provided a pseudointellectual basis for the evil, murder, and prejudice against specific races and women.

> Make no mistake, your worldview affects how you live.

My point: the issue is not a dichotomy of science and God. There are facts that must be faced and implications of classic macroevolution socially and morally that can't be swept under the rug. I want you to ask yourself, which of these truth claims resonates and makes the most sense? I would encourage you to deeply ponder the evidence for yourself.

Question 7: Which theory or claim reflects most accurately the laws of empirical science and research?

Great Scientists' Historical Presuppositions

Great scientists like Newton and da Vinci had presuppositions about order, balance, and predictability. The scientific method grew out of a belief that is absolutely contrary to random chance. Leonardo da Vinci, considered by many to be the real founder of modern science, was believed to be a committed creationist.

Robert Boyle, the father of modern chemistry, was the greatest physical scientist of his generation and an apologist for the Genesis account. Isaac Newton was a prodigious intellect. He developed calculus, discovered the law of gravity, designed the first reflecting telescope, and not only refuted atheism, but he also strongly defended the biblical account of creation.

Louis Pasteur, well known for his process of pasteurization and for utterly demolishing the concept of spontaneous generation, was devoutly religious and strongly opposed to Darwinian evolution.

In the book *Men of Science, Men of God*, Dr. Henry Morris wrote about intellects Kepler, a scientific astronomer; Francis Bacon, developer of the scientific method; Pascal, the mathematician; Linnaeus, taxonomy expert; Mendel, authority on genetics; Faraday, an electromagnetic scientist; and Joseph Lister, leader in antiseptic surgery. He makes the point that these brilliant scientists all had presuppositions. They believed that life had order and that there was a God who gave them wisdom so they could reason. There were predictable constants given by a logical God who wanted you to discover how He made the earth and how it works.[14]

Law of Cause and Effect

Let's think about cause and effect and the second law of thermodynamics. If you walked into your home to find every lamp turned over, the couch upside down, the drawers pulled out, the refrigerator opened, and all your papers all over the floor . . . that's an effect.

Most of you would not say to yourself, "Hmmm, I don't think there's a cause here, it must have been a slight breeze that only came through my house." Or would you say, "I think we've been robbed!"? Especially when you realize that your valuables are gone, your computer is missing from your desk, and your TV is missing from the wall.

Law of Thermodynamics

Cause and effect is one of the most basic laws of science. The Second Law of Thermodynamics says that everything is winding down. If I decide to not cut my grass, will I discover that my lawn has evolved into an immaculate lawn? No, all I get are weeds, and it just looks bad. When I don't take care of my body, I gain weight and I feel lousy. When I don't take time to invest in relationships, they get worse.

When we look at the world around us, we see that it is dying and winding down. Evolution's presupposition says our world is going from chaos to order when, in fact, everything we observe is the exact opposite.

Question 8: Which theory or claim has the best paleontological track record for their position?

As we tackle this last question, I'm reminded of how powerful a belief can become when it goes unchallenged. I remember vividly studying evolution in science class and seeing the

I'm reminded of how powerful a belief can become when it goes unchallenged.

pictures in my textbooks of the progress from apes to mankind. There were actual pictures of one form that gradually turned into another. It was presented as fact. I didn't know they were "made-up drawings." So let's end our time by examining those "facts."

Our "Common Ancestor" and "Missing Links" Discredited

According to macroevolutionary research, apes and humans had a common ancestor, and it was from this missing link or transitioning life-form that our human line developed. Let's highlight the paleontological discoveries for Darwinian macroevolution.

There is Java Man, the name given to early human fossils that scientists believed to be the missing link to modern man. The latest research showed that Java Man had a leg bone that was almost unquestionably human, but the skull has been the topic of much debate. The skull, which was found fifty feet away, was shown to be, most likely, from another creature. Dubois, the man who discovered Java Man, always believed his discovery to be the missing link.[15]

Piltdown Man was discovered by Charles Dawson and presented to the world as the missing link. In this particular case, however, forty-five years later, scientists found that the jawbone was attached artificially to a human skull, that the teeth had been filed down, and that it had been treated with ore to make it appear older.[16]

Then there's the Nebraska Man in 1922. A tooth was found in Nebraska and scientists claimed the tooth could be from the missing link. Scientists later discovered that the tooth was from a pig and it had been misclassified.[17]

Neanderthal Man, discovered near the Neander Valley in Germany, was considered a missing link to modern man. It was promoted in thousands of textbooks and museums. Later it was discovered that it actually walked in a stooped position because it was suffering from diseases and vitamin deficiency. Neanderthal has since been reclassified as Homo sapiens.[18]

In 1964 Lucy, technically an Australopithecus, was believed to be the missing link. Interestingly, Lucy's knee was found two hundred feet lower in the strata and two to three kilometers away from the other bones. When Johanson, the man who discovered Lucy, was questioned during a lecture at the University of Minnesota in 1986 and asked why he thought it belonged to Lucy, his answer was its anatomical similarity. Richard Leakey, well-known evolutionist and director of the National Museum in Kenya, concluded, "It is impossible to draw any firm conclusion about what species Lucy belongs to."[19]

Scientists continue to look for transitional fossils (called the missing link when I grew up) and gather evidence of our early human ancestors. Some believe human fossils found in Africa and in the country of Georgia over the last few years are part of modern man's family tree. As scientists study these remains, new theories emerge of how our ancestors lived and what they were like.

So, how do those "pictures" in my ninth-grade textbook stand against the facts? Could it be that our human nature is so anxious to be free from God that we're willing to be anti-intellectual to believe a theory with gaps, holes, and socially evil consequences?

The Biblical Archaeological Track Record

For me personally, I believe in the historical, literal, grammatical, biblical account of creation. I also believe that scientists will continue to search for the missing link, from ape to mankind. I think it is logical to assume they will develop new theories, but they will never find what they are looking for. History would argue that both the Bible's historical and archaeological accuracy are unsurpassed. No discovery has disproved the biblical accounts to date. We have over twenty-five thousand archaeological connections in the Old Testament alone, of actual people, places, and events. So, when I look at archaeology and the historical accounts in the Bible, does it measure up? In comparison to the paleontologists' search for the missing links, I would say that the Bible is clearly superior. I've never seen where science and the Bible contradict, but I have certainly seen where our biblical interpretations and scientific interpretations radically conflict.

I have met many people who identify as followers of Christ and are very negative toward science. They don't want to study or examine any other idea that may be different than their own. We should be the kind of Christ follower who says, you know what? We may not understand everything that is happening in science, but we are going to learn, grow, stay informed, and be ready to give a kind, honest, and intellectually astute answer for the hope we have in Christ and the amazing world He made that makes science possible. We are going to listen to and show love to people who may disagree with us.

> As Christ followers, we are going to listen to and show love to people who may disagree with us.

Final Questions

I want to leave you with a few questions to ponder. Not just for you and me, but for the people whom we care about.

1. Is Darwinian evolution really the airtight scientific fact that we were led to believe it was and were taught in school? Think about that and think about the implications for your view of God, justice, and the value of every human life.

2. Should the recent scientific discoveries among top non-Christian scientists cause us to reexamine our view of Darwinian evolution's validity?

3. Could Darwinian evolution be the intellectual justification for racism, Nazism, sexism, and moral relativism? Could you defend Darwinian philosophy applied to those areas?

4. And finally, what do you believe personally? What do you believe about the origin of life? And why? Based upon what? Does your life demonstrate intellectual consistency with what you say you believe? That's really the big issue.

We covered a lot of ground and I hope that I haven't over-whelmed you. Yet when I think back to my conversation with the brilliant young man in my kitchen who assumed believing in God and a Creator was antithetical to being a scientist, I want to scream, "That's a false dichotomy!"

This chapter summarizes why I am a thinking, analytical, scientifically oriented follower of Jesus who has come to the intellectual and faith conclusion that life is best explained by a personal God who created, rather than the result of random chance over billions of years.

8

Why I Believe in the God of the Bible

> This is what the LORD says—
>> Israel's King and Redeemer, the Lord Almighty:
> I am the first and I am the last;
>> apart from me there is no God.
> Who then is like me? Let him proclaim it.
>> Let him declare and lay out before me
> what has happened since I established my ancient
>> people,
>> and what is yet to come—
>> yes, let them foretell what will come.
>
> Isaiah 44:6–7

About six months ago I was walking from one end of our church building to the other on a Sunday morning. The hallways were crowded with children going to their classes and parents doing their best to make it down to the worship center. As I briskly made my way through the controlled chaos, an Asian couple caught my eye. I couldn't tell whether they were lost or simply deep in thought as children and passersby filed on either side of them.

I was prompted to stop and introduce myself and ask them a few questions. Within minutes they told me a story that is not unique in our church, as we have many nationalities from many backgrounds. "We have been coming to this church for a number of months and exploring the claims of Jesus and Christianity. We see the impact on our children, the warmth of these people, and the intellectual clarity and historical basis of your teaching. We are very grateful that we have never felt pushed in any way but have had time to explore, examine, and ask questions about what it really means to be a follower of Jesus Christ. My wife has accepted and trusted in Jesus as her Savior and Lord, and I'm on the verge of doing the same, but we return to our homeland for the holidays and we are carefully weighing the implications of making this decision. We come from a family of several generations of Buddhists. We would be betraying our ancestors, and our decision would communicate that they were wrong. There will be a significant price to becoming followers of Jesus."

As we turn the corner on our final leg of this journey together, one of the most unpopular but important issues to address is why I believe in the God of the Bible.

There are over 320 million gods to choose from and 22 world religions, each with at least a half million followers.[1] With so many options, how do we know who is the true God? Is it intellectually feasible to believe that there is one true God, the God of the Bible, and all the others are wrong? Doesn't that sound a little narrow? Is such a position even remotely defensible? If so, what evidence supports such an outlandish claim?

Before you begin to process those questions, let me ask you to explore two important presuppositions. First, we'll revisit the term *presupposition*—a conscious or unconscious assumption about what is true or how we view the world. In other words, it's something we assume without even thinking. It is what our culture has taught us. It's what we've heard so often that we assume it to be true. As a result, presuppositions become the basis for our values, decision making, and thinking about life. Presuppositions are like the invisible foundations of our reasoning and values. You don't see the foundation of the house, but everything is built upon it; and correspondingly, if the foundation is faulty, everything built upon it will be as well.

> Presuppositions are like the invisible foundations of our reasoning and values.

So let's look at a couple very common presuppositions before we consider what I shared with the former Buddhist family in that hallway.

The first presupposition is that all religions are essentially the same. Many believe that all religions worship the same god but give god different names and worship in different ways.

Gandhi said it this way: "The soul of religion is one, but it is encased in a multitude of forms."[2] Another way of describing it goes like this: There is a holy mountain with many paths providing a way to the top of the mountain. All humanity is on one of the paths to the top. Some take the Buddhist path, some Hinduism, some Shintoism, some Taoism, some Christianity, some Islam, some Judaism, and some New Age. But when we make it to the top, we will all meet god and we will realize he was just known by many different names.

This popular explanation seems to be nice, inclusive, and loving, but it actually demonstrates a significant lack of understanding and could even be considered insulting to most of the world's religions.

If I could put a group of seven or eight people together and include experts in Buddhism, Hinduism, Islam, Judaism, Jehovah's Witnesses, Mormons, and Shintoism, let me tell you what they would adamantly say: "No, you don't understand. That is not what we believe." Now, maybe the person at the far end, the Bahaist, would actually agree with everybody on everything, and we could probably get a New Ager to say, "We feel good about that." But the truth is that all religions aren't the same. To say they are all basically the same is not intellectually consistent. It is like saying that black, white, red, and purple are all the same color. No, they are not all the same color. These various belief systems are radically different in who they purport God to be, even if they use the same name.

The second presupposition is that it really doesn't matter what a person believes as long as he or she sincerely practices those beliefs.

We live in a very pluralistic society today. To say that only one religious belief is right actually makes you sound intolerant, narrow-minded, anti-intellectual, and uncaring. Popular belief holds that what is good and right for me may not be good or right for you, and that is okay as long as we are sincere about our beliefs.

A common thread between Islam, Judaism, Buddhism, and almost every major religion is that they have high regard for Jesus. All of these religions see Him as a loving, good, moral teacher. They do not identify Jesus as the Son of God, the second person of the Trinity, or the Savior of the world, but they all agree that He is an example of how people ought to live. He is the ideal of love. But according to Jesus, the most loving person, it *does* matter what you believe. He said,

> Enter through the narrow gate. For wide is the gate and broad is the road that leads to destruction, and many enter through it. But small is the gate and narrow the road that leads to life, and only a few find it. (Matt. 7:13–14)

Sincerity as the highest value sounds compassionate, kind, and nonjudgmental. But let's follow that logic into other areas of life. Say you have a very sick child and you go to the pharmacist to pick up a prescription. The pharmacist, with sincere intentions, fills the wrong prescription and your child dies. If the pharmacist had sincerely wanted to help, can you be upset with him or her? It was just a different drug, and it didn't work. No harm was intended. Who are you to judge the pharmacist?

Or how about if your mate, during an exceptionally hard or busy season of your marriage, gets emotionally attracted to or physically involved with another person? What if your mate walks out on you because of deep, sincere feelings for another person? After all, they are only following their heart and being true to themselves. Isn't it okay because they're being sincere? Does feeling sincere and good about something justify it?

We would never allow sincerity to override truth in other areas of our lives. It is all too easy to withdraw when we find ourselves in discussions about God with family, friends, or coworkers, worrying that they will think we are anti-intellectual, narrow-minded, or hateful. But, when you know truth, backing away or withdrawing from the conversation is the epitome of being unloving.

We hide behind sincerity because we don't want to be rejected. Jesus loved people so much that He told them the truth in love. Jesus said, "I am the way and the truth and the life. No one comes to the Father except through me" (John 14:6).

Moving past these presuppositions, let's now look at the evidence behind why I believe the God of the Bible is the one true God. There are seven reasons why I believe in the God of the Bible. Each reason could be a book in itself. In fact, volumes have been written about each of these reasons by experts in the field. But what I hope to share with you is the larger landscape in order for you to grasp a macroscopic view of this most critical topic. I often find that people dig into the

> These pillars support the intellectually compelling conclusion that there is only one true God.

details and get caught up in so many specific issues that they lose sight of the major pillars of truth. These pillars support the intellectually compelling conclusion that there is only one true God. At the end of our discussion in chapter 9, you will find that I've listed a number of specific resources that will help you explore at a deeper level what I will summarize in these two chapters (see page 209).

Reason #1: Historical Evidence

I believe in the God of the Bible because of historical evidence. As we have already learned in chapters 1 and 2, the people, places, and documentation of biblical events have been verified by archaeology.

We have also learned what the Bible says is reliable. Far from oral legends or myths handed down from one generation to the other, we have thousands of documents and fragments that demonstrate a supernatural, accurate transmission of the Bible, which include the Dead Sea Scrolls and the New Testament manuscripts written by real people in real times that we can document.

Most religious truth claims have spiritual leaders who have had unverifiable dreams or experiences they claim to be from God. By contrast, Christianity is rooted in actual historical events authenticated by secular historians that validate the existence of Jesus, His claims, and the early teaching and actions of His followers in the first century. The Greek historian Pliny, the Jewish historian Josephus, and the Roman historian Tacitus all provide external verification of Jesus in early Christianity.

Christianity is subject to objective verification.

I don't have to base my faith, my life, and my future on one of many possible religions that claim to be true. I can verify and evaluate the evidence for Christianity. I can go to the place where Jesus lived and study historically verified, first-century documents. Christianity is subject to objective verification.

Reason #2: Prophetic Evidence

The specific fulfillment of specific events foretold supports the God of the Bible. In chapter 2, we saw that biblical prophecies weren't vague patterns of things that might happen someday. The Bible predicted specific future events with 100 percent accuracy.

Throughout history, many religions have claimed that their beliefs are true. During the time of Isaiah, people worshiped many gods. Listen to what the God of the Bible said in Isaiah 44:6–7:

> This is what the LORD says—
>   Israel's King and Redeemer, the LORD Almighty:
> I am the first and I am the last;
>   apart from me there is no God.
> Who then is like me? Let him proclaim it.
>   Let him declare and lay out before me
> what has happened since I established my ancient
>   people,
>   and what is yet to come—
>   yes, let them foretell what will come.

172

God began His challenge to all other "gods" by establishing His authority as YAHWEH, the I AM. That is a very narrow claim, and He gives proof to back His claim. Let's take a look at His supporting evidence in Isaiah 44:24–28:

> This is what the LORD says—
>> your Redeemer, who formed you in the womb:
> I am the LORD,
>> the Maker of all things,
>> who stretches out the heavens,
>> who spreads out the earth by myself,
> who foils the signs of false prophets
>> and makes fools of diviners,
> who overthrows the learning of the wise
>> and turns it into nonsense,
> who carries out the words of his servants
>> and fulfills the predictions of his messengers,
>
> who says of Jerusalem, "It shall be inhabited,"
>> of the towns of Judah, "They shall be rebuilt"
>> and of their ruins, "I will restore them,"
> who says to the watery deep, "Be dry,
>> and I will dry up your streams,"
> who says of Cyrus, "He is my shepherd
>> and will accomplish all that I please;
> he will say of Jerusalem, 'Let it be rebuilt,'
>> and of the temple, 'Let its foundations be laid.'"

God's supporting evidence for His authority is that He is the Creator. He spoke and all that is came to be. He is the Redeemer. He is the Lord—the *Almighty*. He is the all-powerful One. He challenged all the other "gods" to an authenticity test. The test was to predict the future with absolute accuracy. Only the one true God could do that.

Deuteronomy 18:21–22 gives us the way to test a true prophet of God:

> You may say to yourselves, "How can we know when a message has not been spoken by the Lord?" If what a prophet proclaims in the name of the Lord does not take place or come true, that is a message the Lord has not spoken. That prophet has spoken presumptuously, so do not be alarmed.

Then God gave Isaiah a very specific prediction about the deliverance of His people to establish His authority as the one true God. God told Isaiah that He foreordained a man named Cyrus to break Babylonian rule, free the children of Israel, and establish the timeline for the coming of the Messiah. Nearly 150 years later, Cyrus the Great was born and everything happened just as God said it would. Isaiah was a true prophet of God, and we can trust that his message was from God.

How many world religions have made predictions that haven't come true? And we just gloss over them. How many people make promises about what will happen out of their religious systems? And they don't come true.

As for me, I can evaluate objectively and verify the claims of the God that I believe in. I have prophetic evidence and the fulfillment of hundreds of specific promises and predictions in the Bible.

Reason #3: Philosophical Evidence

I believe the biblical worldview and the triune nature of God as communicated in the Bible provide the most satisfying answers to mankind's age-old philosophical questions. Every religion or truth claim must grapple with and answer these basic questions:

- How does the world fit together?
- What is the relationship between unity and diversity in the cosmos?
- What is the source of evil and suffering?
- What is the source of personhood?
- What separates man from the animals and why?
- Is mankind basically good or evil?
- How is human progress and virtue to be understood in view of violence, cruelty, and genocide?

These are the age-old questions about which volumes have been written; but let me attempt to provide a thumbnail sketch on a portion of them to help you begin to see the wisdom and unique worldview that the God of the Bible provides.

The Problem of Unity and Diversity

For centuries people have tried to explain the unity and diversity in the world. How can both coexist in the universe? Some beliefs choose to focus on unity. They hold that the ultimate state of being is oneness with nature and the universe, to be at harmony with the god within and/or with the created order. Buddhism and New Age teaching fall into this category.

Others focus on diversity. The Egyptian, Roman, and Greek gods reflected the diversity seen in the world. They consistently changed loyalties and battled each other for control, never finding unity.

Christianity is the only religious system that has by definition both unity and diversity through the nature of the Godhead. There is one God, one Essence, and three personalities. You have unity and diversity, nature and the cosmos reflected in His character.

> Therefore go and make disciples of all nations, baptizing them in the name [singular] of the Father and of the Son and of the Holy Spirit. (Matt. 28:19)

There is one God, one Essence, and three personalities.

Note that when Jesus commanded His followers to make disciples of all nations, He told them to baptize them in the *name* (singular) of the Father, Son, and Holy Spirit (plural). For those with a philosophical bent who would like to explore this further, I would recommend Francis Schaeffer's work in *The God Who Is There*, *He Is There and He Is Not Silent*, and *Escape from Reason*.

The Problem of Evil and Justice

The problem of evil is a huge issue to address. I am often asked how a good God could allow evil in the world. People doubt God's goodness when they look around and see children starving, loved ones dying of cancer, and the horrendous killing of innocent people. This question is a challenge to every religion and philosophy.

There are religious systems whose god is both good and evil. Many religions are fear based because there is no assurance of salvation or remaining in the god's favor. Historically, much of religion has been aimed at appeasing an angry god or ancestors who have died. Not so with Christianity.

> This is the message we have heard from him and declare to you: God is light; in him there is no darkness at all. (1 John 1:5)

The God of the Bible is an absolutely good God (Mark 10:18), who created an absolutely good and pure world (Gen. 1:31). God, in His goodness, created a perfect world for mankind but allowed man the freedom to choose to love Him or reject Him. The Bible calls this self-centered rebellion sin. Sin (evil) entered the world through Adam, forever changing the nature of mankind (Rom. 5:12). We have a good, loving, patient, and sovereign God who is seeking to restore mankind to a loving relationship with Himself and who offers redemption and forgiveness in God the Son on the cross. We are living in a fallen, morally corrupt world that was not His ideal. One day He promises to make all things right (2 Pet. 3:9). But until that day comes, He actively purposes to redeem the evil and painful circumstances in our lives.

It's interesting to see that God sets aside a third of the book of Genesis to tell the story of the life of Joseph. Joseph was his father's favorite son, and he was one of twelve brothers. He dreamed that he would one day have a position of authority over his family. When he shared his dream with his brothers, they sold him into slavery. After years of slavery, false accusations of rape, and imprisonment, God used Joseph to help Egypt not only survive, but thrive through a serious famine. Years later, Joseph was able to bless his brothers instead of retaliating for the way they treated him, realizing God used their evil intent to save the nation of Israel.

Why would the account of Joseph's life be given more chapters in Genesis than anyone else's story? God did this so that we can clearly see His goodness and sovereignty in the midst of a fallen world and find true hope in Him. What happens to the injustice of bad and partial parenting? What happens to the injustice of rejection? What happens to the injustice of slavery? What happens when you're falsely accused? What happens when you are unjustly put in prison? What happens when you are forgotten? This is Joseph's perspective through the lens of God's sovereign goodness:

> Biblical Christianity offers hope and redemption in a fallen world.

> You intended to harm me, but God intended it for good to accomplish what is now being done, the saving of many lives. (Gen. 50:20)

In a fallen and sinful world, people use, betray, hurt, and abuse one another. God does not necessarily prevent these acts of evil (though at times He supernaturally intervenes), but in His goodness, God uses painful circumstances in our lives for the greater good in our life or in the lives of others. This is a very unique and amazing worldview that no other religious system shares. It addresses the reason for suffering and separates God the Creator from the evil in the world. Unlike the fatalism of many religions or the endless cycles of retribution for evil in others, biblical Christianity offers hope and redemption in a fallen world. For a more thorough examination of this topic, I recommend *The Problem of Pain* by C. S. Lewis.

The Origin of Personality

Personality comes out of personhood. Multiple religious systems claim that there is no personality, only oneness with the universe. Others believe that our personality is just a by-product of an evolutionary process and our DNA. Our likes and dislikes are programmed, not a personal choice.

> So God created mankind in his own image, in the image of God he created them; male and female he created them. (Gen. 1:27)

The God of the Bible is a personal God who lovingly created us (Ps. 139). Early theologians, followed later by the leaders of the Reformation, called this idea the *Imago Dei*. Humanity is made in the image of God. We are the pinnacle of God's creation, possessing dignity and grandeur. We are not merely animals, living by animal instinct for the moment. We were created for more than survival. We above all the life-forms on earth can think, love, and create. We have meaning and purpose in life.

The Enigma of Man

How can mankind be so intelligent, noble, and creative, yet be so cruel and inhumane? Over the last hundred years we have seen the most amazing advancements in technology, medicine, and communication and yet witnessed more bloodshed than any other century in all of history. The answer, scripturally, is that we are made in the image of God (dignity) and yet we live as fallen human beings (cruelty), which requires a Savior.

> So I find this law at work: Although I want to do good, evil is right there with me. For in my inner being I delight

in God's law; but I see another law at work in me, waging war against the law of my mind and making me a prisoner of the law of sin at work within me. What a wretched man I am! Who will rescue me from this body that is subject to death? Thanks be to God, who delivers me through Jesus Christ our Lord! (Rom. 7:21–25)

Biblical Christianity best answers the question of man's greatness and potential for almost unimaginable evil. Scripture describes with graphic detail the conflict of the human heart and the struggle to live above the base impulses of greed and jealousy that lead to violence.

Reason #4: The Evidence of Positive World Impact

Every religion exacts some measure of impact on the culture and world around it. Some religions have created endless cycles of retribution through a belief in reincarnation and developed caste systems and systematic poverty. Other religions promote violence to all non-adherants and subjugate women as second-class citizens unable to get an education, vote, or even drive a car in some parts of the world today. Although it is a highly pragmatic argument, I believe in the God of the Bible in some measure because of its massive and sustained positive impact in the world.

To be sure, like any religion, some misguided followers have used their belief in the God of the Bible to exact suffering and injustice upon others; but the overwhelming evidence that flows from a good God whose message is one of love and redemption for all people regardless of their race, gender, or personal failures is one of astounding positive impact.

My friend and fellow teaching pastor at Venture Christian Church is John S. Dickerson. He is a nationally awarded journalist.[3] His work has been published in the *New York Times* and *USA Today*, among others.[4] As a skeptic, John set out to investigate Christianity. He wanted to learn if Christianity has been a force for good or for evil.

In his forthcoming book, *Jesus Skeptic*, John describes how surprised he was by the impact of Christianity. After gathering and analyzing the evidence about Christianity, just as he would for a news investigation, John found the following:

> To understand the impact of Christianity, I realized that I first needed to understand what life was like before Jesus "the Christ" was born. Today, about one-in-three people in the world identify as Christian. Having inherited such a Christian-influenced world, it is hard to grasp what life was like before Christianity.
>
> Historians and artifacts agree about the bleak and difficult lives most humans experienced prior to the birth of Jesus. Average life expectancy was 30 to 40 years. It was a world without electricity or modern medicine, a world in which most people were illiterate and uneducated. It was a world where slavery was common on every continent, and where the majority of people who escaped slavery lived as peasants, in a hand-to-mouth existence "little better off than their oxen."
>
> Most people never owned land, never had a bank account, and never learned to read. They had no antibiotics, no serious painkillers, and no scientifically informed doctors. Women were routinely killed as infants (because girls were less desirable than boys), and those girls who survived were often traded as property. Disease, plague and famine could strike and kill at any time. It was a violent and brutal world ruled

by a few powerful people and their armies, a world without democracy or human rights as we know them today.

The world we have inherited is far different from history's global norm, and so we must ask: "What happened?" *Why did the world change so dramatically after Jesus? Who instigated the advances that doubled life expectancy? Who worked to increase literacy from 2 percent to nearly 100 percent in the U.S.A. and Western Europe? Who launched modern science? Who abolished slavery, and why?*

If we trace backwards through history, we can find the undeniable sources beneath each of these human improvements. We can produce artifacts and documentation which prove where these improvements find their origin. And, we can learn what motivated the people who changed the course of history for the better.

> Sincere Christians, motivated by their faith in Jesus, had instigated the world-changing social improvements we take for granted today.
> —John Dickerson

I was shocked to discover—again and again—that sincere Christians, motivated by their faith in Jesus, had instigated the world-changing social improvements we take for granted today. Here's a summary of some evidence compiled in my book, *Jesus Skeptic*.

The seeds of modern science, medicine and democracy all began, it turns out, with Christian education. Specifically, they all trace to early Christian "Monastic schools," which began spreading around Europe in the early AD 300s (or ACE).

The Monastic Schools then gave birth to Cathedral Schools, which Christians operated in dozens of European cities from the AD 500s. These Christian schools formed the spine of today's K–12 education and many remain in existence today. Around AD 1000, Christian cathedrals began offering further education for the graduates of their Cathedral schools. This gave birth to a unique learning institution called the *universita*, from the Latin word meaning "the whole, total, or the universe."

The universita was the dramatic fork in the road for human development—specifically its permission to study everything. For thousands of years, other civilizations had had synagogues and temple places of learning, but the Christian universitas became something different. They transformed education from rote memorization to intellectual exploration. They incubated intellectual stimulation, gave students permission to question authority, and introduced "deductive reasoning" into the classroom.

Based on the foundational belief that God is good, predictable, truthful, and orderly, everything in the universe became fair game to be explored, tested, and dissected. Classrooms of students who had already learned the basics in their Cathedral schools could now add layers of scientific, mathematical, medical, and theological exploration.

Many of those early Christian universitas grew up around the stone cathedral churches in European cities—which is why the architecture at the world's best universities continues to mimic cathedral church architecture to this day. At nearly 1,000 years old, the University of Oxford began as one of these early Christian universitas. With its scriptural motto "The Lord is My Light," Oxford remains among the oldest and most renowned universities in the world.

The Light of the Lord, as Oxford's motto phrases it, began shining into the darkness of ignorance. Scientific learning commenced. Independent thought flourished. Compassionate ethics leaped forward. Brave ideas about how Christ's teaching could better shape a future society took root.

Tracing artifacts and records back through history, it becomes clear that Christian universities like Oxford provided the intellectual foundations of modern science, medicine, education, democracy, and more.

Within education, Oxford is frequently cited as a father of the modern university because so many of the world's most renowned universities trace back to it. For example, in the year 1209 Oxford gave birth to Cambridge. Later, a graduate of Cambridge—the Reverend John Harvard—helped start a college known today as Harvard University.

Like its counterparts Yale and Princeton, Harvard was started by a group of Christian pastors, in order to train young Christians to read the Christian Scriptures. This is all clearly documented in the historic record and founding documents of these schools. Examine the highest ranked universities in the world today, and you will find their founders and early faculty to be graduates from Harvard, Yale, Princeton, Cambridge, Oxford, and other early Christian-initiated universities.

The impact of these schools is more dramatic than I can explain. For example, devout Christian graduates from Cambridge, valuing the need for every Christian to be able to read the Christian Bible personally, launched a world-changing law requiring towns to provide free education to all children. At the time, less than 5 percent of the people in the world could read. That law is today considered the cornerstone of public education and literacy. It was the turning point from a world in which most people could not read to a world where most can. As a result, you are able to read the words on this page.

An educated public produced further advances in science, medicine, industry, continued education, and even the formation of new governments. These advancements sprouted exclusively in Christian regions of the world, which were home to Christian universities and schools like Harvard and Oxford. Within generations of the law requiring public schools and literacy, graduates of these early universities founded the United States of America. All this fruit grew from the original seed of Oxford and the early Christian universitas.

These Christian-founded universities shaped, educated, and produced the graduates who undeniably:

- Launched the Scientific Revolution
- Launched the Industrial Revolution
- Created the first society in which girls were provided equal education to boys
- Created the first society in which all people were taught to read—thus planting the seed of a literate public
- Created and spread Western democracy as we know and enjoy it today
- Invented eyeglasses and thousands of other life-changing inventions
- Discovered the laws of planetary motion
- Discovered germ theory and other innovations that launched modern medicine
- Created modern hospitals
- Eradicated disease
- Created life-saving vaccines, which have saved millions of lives
- Fought for women's rights
- Abolished slavery first in Christianized Europe, then in Christian England, and then in the United States. Only after slavery was abolished in Christianized

Europe and North America did the abolishment of slavery spread as a norm and human right to the rest of the world.

- Exported these improvements around the world, thus improving humanity in ways we cannot fully grasp or measure

It's not merely that the men and women who changed history in these ways had been shaped by Christian universities or schools. That is fact, and that fact alone would be a significant accomplishment for Christianity. But the reality—as I dug deeper—is that so many of the men and women who instigated these leaps forward were motivated by their personal Christian faith. They were men and women who truly believed that Jesus was God, that Jesus died on the cross for the sins of the world, and that faith in Jesus leads to an eternal life. Their belief that God loves people and created an orderly universe led them to their breakthroughs in hospital care, medicine, human rights, science, and the abolishing of slavery.

Imagine a world in which you and I have a life expectancy of 40 years, have no modern medicine, cannot read, cannot vote, and do not have any electric or mechanical accessories. Imagine living in a society where babies are still cast onto the compost heap when they are unwanted, where humans are sold as slaves in open markets, and where women are treated like property.

Remove the Christian institutions and individuals above, and we would be living in such a world. This is not my opinion. These are real people like William Wilberforce, Florence Nightingale, John Harvard, Frederick Douglass, and many others, whose lives and writings can be examined. I invite you to study each of them for yourself.

In fact, if you look at a world map showing life expectancy, literacy, women's rights, and other issues, you will see that the historically Christian nations lead the world in these improvements, while the nations most opposed to Christianity still lag far behind in gender rights, life expectancy, literacy, and even slavery (with some Muslim and Hindu regions that prohibit Christianity still having slaves in our lifetime).

> Many of the men and women who instigated these leaps forward were motivated by their personal Christian faith.
>
> —John Dickerson

For one example of Christianity's influence in these human gains, let's look at the Scientific Revolution. Famous scientists Isaac Newton, Johannes Kepler, and Blaise Pascal unlocked the secrets of the universe. Each of these men were so devoted in their Christian faith that they wrote personal prayers and Christian Scriptures in their journals. Those documents remain to this day and can be investigated. In a note which Blaise Pascal kept in his coat, he wrote, "This is eternal life, that they know you, the one true God, and the one that you sent, Jesus Christ." Pascal, of course, remains one of the most important scientific fathers in history.

Isaac Newton, also among the most influential scientists of all time, wrote thousands of pages about Jesus and Christianity. You can read them today, including this line from one of his journals: "Christ gave himself for me."

PhD sociologist Rodney Stark explored journals and artifacts from the 52 most influential scientists who launched the Scientific Revolution. Dr. Stark found that 60 percent of them were devout Christians—of the passion shared by Newton and Pascal. Another 38 percent of the scientific fathers were sincere, formal Christians who consistently attended church. Within the accepted fathers of modern science, only 2 percent are documented skeptics of Christianity.

Very simply put, the fathers of modern science were Christians who were educated by Christian universities, and they

> The fathers of modern science were Christians who were educated by Christian universities, and they routinely credited their Christian faith as the reason for their breakthroughs in discovery.
> —John Dickerson

routinely credited their Christian faith as the reason for their breakthroughs in discovery. Examine the founders of modern medicine, education, democracy, philanthropy, women's suffrage, the abolition of slavery, and you will find the same trend: Christians, educated by Christians, changing the world because of Christianity's ideas.

Dig through the evidence yourself, as I did (and I've documented it for you in the *Jesus Skeptic* book), and you will find that Christians continually pop up as the instigators of these movements which have so foundationally improved human life.

As a skeptic and an investigative journalist, I have come to the following conclusion. I draw this conclusion from having examined the actual evidence.

Sincere Christians, motivated by their Christian faith, have improved humanity more than any other single group. Indisputable, primary evidence demonstrates plainly that Christians invented or instigated the following:

- Universities and colleges that lifted civilization from ignorance to intelligence
- Specific "seed" institutions such as Oxford, Cambridge, Harvard, Yale, Princeton, and Johns Hopkins, which birthed the world's most significant universities, hospitals, inventors, physicians, educators, and champions of human rights

- Widespread literacy
- Public education
- Western democracy
- Education for women as well as men
- The abolition of slavery
- Unprecedented women's rights
- Modern philanthropy including Catholic and other Christian hospitals
- Public charity as a societal norm and large charitable institutions, which care for the poor, homeless, and widows, including Christian-initiated organizations like The Salvation Army, Goodwill, the YMCA (Young Men's Christian Association), and many more
- The Scientific Revolution and its resulting improvements for billions by preventing famine and waterborne disease, among other improvements
- Germ theory, sterile practice, and modern medicine
- Hospitals and modern nursing as we know them
- Vaccines and the hundreds of millions of lives they have saved

It is not a leap to say that if these advances were removed from history, then you and I would be living in a world much closer to the barbaric, brutal, and ignorant peasant world that held humanity captive for so many thousands of years. Remove these Christians above, and you remove the benefits above. These innovations did not spring up in Buddhist, Muslim, pagan, or other societies. Somehow, for some reason, these advancements sprung up from overwhelmingly Christian-educated innovators. To me, that is notable.

This led me to a bold but undeniable conclusion:

Whether I personally like Christianity or not, whether I believe its spiritual claims or not, Christianity bears studying, for it has been—by multiple measures—the most viral movement for social good in all of human history.[5]

(John invites any who disagree with his conclusion to examine the primary evidence, which will be documented in his book *Jesus Skeptic*, available Spring 2019.)

As my friend John found, Christianity has impacted our world in undeniable ways. You'll note that John footnoted each of those claims because his conclusions are based on many hours of research of primary sources. You can examine them for yourself, as they are available in the endnotes.

Here is another disclaimer. There are some wonderful exceptions of quality biblical teaching on television; however, much of the teaching on "Christian TV" misrepresents who Jesus is and what He taught. Many of these teachers make outrageous claims and financially plunder people. Their actions disenfranchise unbelievers from the true gospel, and I pray that non-Christians never see these teachers. As Christ followers, one of the things we struggle with in our day is how to get through that clutter to say, "This is who God really is and what true followers of Jesus are." Nevertheless, if one steps back and looks at the history of Israel and the work of the church over the last 4,000 years, it has had a staggering influence of good for the world. Let me share just a few examples to help you grasp what I'm talking about.

A few thousand years ago, God chose a man named Abraham to make a great nation through which He would bless the world. God kept that promise and He continues to bless the world to this day. The amazing journey from a nomad in a tent, to a nation, to the Law, to King David, to Solomon, to where Israel is today is nothing short of miraculous. Only a sovereign and all-powerful God could be behind it.

The laws that God gave to the Israelites have transformed our world. The Ten Commandments are the most widely recognized rules on how to treat people, whether you follow them or not. God also gave the Israelites rules governing hygiene and washing. It makes sense that the Creator of the universe and all-knowing God gave medically accurate advice for disease control, communal sanitation, and the prevention of spreading germs.

We take for granted the time and place we live in. We can forget the effect that an itinerant preacher made on the world two thousand years ago. Jesus radically changed the world one person at a time. Christianity grew from a tiny mustard seed of a few hundred followers to an estimated two billion followers worldwide today. Though practiced imperfectly, followers of Jesus have emulated His life, His love, and His teaching for the good of others. Jesus' promise of peace and choosing to love one's enemies has restored homes, stopped wars, built schools, created hospitals, and cared for orphans.

Every day, people all over the world are putting their faith in Christ. It is estimated that hundreds of thousands of Muslims become followers of Jesus every year and more have placed their faith in Jesus during the twenty-first century compared to any other time in history. Fenggang Yang, a professor of sociology at Purdue University, predicts that if the number of Christians continues to grow as it is now, the followers of Jesus in China will exceed 247 million people by the year 2030. In Africa, over the last fifteen years alone, an average of 33,000 people became Christians every day. Many of these people face horrendous persecution, but they continue to follow Jesus. As the church grows, life and love follows. Forgiveness is extended to others and integrity replaces corruption. In a world that offers so little hope to those who are marginalized, the impact of Christians living out their faith for good continues to expand.

Around the world, millions of Christians are making a difference in the lives of people. Christian relief organizations like Samaritan's Purse are first responders at hurricanes, floods, and tsunamis, bringing food, clothing, and the love of Christ. Ministries like the International Justice Mission and hundreds like them are delivering women and children from the sex trade and slavery all around the world. Even a casual look at India and Africa would reveal that schools, hospitals, and orphanages have been started and are maintained by Christians meeting the deepest needs of people in poverty and crisis. My friends at Mercy Ships have floating hospitals with top-level surgeons and medical care that port in the world's most underprivileged regions, treating Muslims, Buddhists, Hindus, and anyone in need.

Thousands of churches all across America and the world do similar work, like our church here in the Silicon Valley. We support or have started forty-two local ministries that minister to the homeless, to those with drug, alcohol, and sexual addictions, and to those with unplanned pregnancies, as well as partnering with the local government to clean, paint, and help remodel local schools. We then support and encourage the teachers and provide tutoring and after-school care for students with special needs. In India and Africa we have a twenty-year track record of supporting hundreds of children and developing schools that provide not only education but job training to become financially self-sufficient, all in the name of Christ. In South Africa we help sponsor orphanages, train pastors, and minister to babies that are HIV-positive. Last year we gave over $2 million or roughly 20 percent of our budget to meet the needs of those outside of our church.

I do not say this to boast in any way—our church is just a typical example of what Christian churches are doing here and all around the world to impact people, governments, and nations for good.

There have certainly been negative things done in the name of God and Christianity, but the massive evidence both today and historically is that followers of Jesus have overwhelmingly impacted our world for good.

As I talked to the young Buddhist couple in that hallway at church, I knew they were facing a monumental decision. The historical, prophetic, and philosophical evidence we have covered in this chapter, along with the impact that Jesus is having through His body (the church) in their lives provided them with more than enough intellectual "evidence" to choose to receive and follow Jesus. But despite our insistence that we think things through logically and need to evaluate the "evidence," the pull of tradition and the concern of what others think powerfully shape our behavior.

As you ponder what you really believe and where you stand with Jesus, what challenges are you currently facing? What tradition, fear, or relationships hold you back from boldly acknowledging that Jesus is the way, the truth, and the life? What more evidence do you require to align your thinking, lifestyle, priorities, and resources to follow the one true God?

I would like you to consider pausing for a few minutes, grab a cup of coffee or your favorite tea, and really ponder the answer to those questions. Deep, protracted thinking always precedes significant life-changing behavior. You owe it to yourself to really STOP and THINK. Refuse to skim, or continue to buy in to the current presuppositions of our age. Take some time before you read the next chapter to ask yourself, "What do I really believe and why?"

9

How's That Working for You?

I am not a big daytime TV watcher, but I have caught Dr. Phil on more than a few occasions. If you're not familiar with the program, he is a counselor who does actual counseling on TV with people who have unique and complex relational issues and problems.

He's known for his direct approach that helps people confront their denial and face their challenges. He nearly always provides ongoing counseling or financial help for the people on his program if they're willing to receive it. What I appreciate most is his loving but no-nonsense approach to helping people face the reality of their situation. After showing taped interviews of their life issues, interaction with other family members, and enough information for everyone but the counselee to see the real problem, he asks this pivotal question, "So how's that working for you?"

It usually happens about halfway through the program after the person continues to explain how their eating disorder, sexual or alcohol addiction, codependency, or out-of-control spending really isn't a problem. In other words, he takes them out of their mental perspective of their life situation and forces them to ask the pragmatic question, how is this working for you? The obvious implication is that if it was working well for them, then they probably wouldn't be on the program.

As we wrap up our time together, I would like to address the Dr. Phil question as it relates to Jesus and Christianity. So, how's that working for you?

Reason #5: Pragmatic Evidence

Pragmatic evidence is the fifth reason that I believe in the God of the Bible. Jesus' teaching works in real life! Pragmatism alone isn't great evidence, but when partnered with the other evidences we have looked at, it strengthens my belief that the God of the Bible is the one true God.

Jesus' teaching promotes healthy relationships, strong marriages, honest businesses, positive parenting, racial reconciliation, and cultural kindness. His teaching champions the value and dignity of all human beings, regardless of creed, race, sex, nationality, or orientation. Christians don't have to agree with people's behavior or beliefs to love and care for them.

Our world is being torn apart by hatred and anger. Jesus calls His followers to be agents of love! Jesus said in John 13:34–35, "A new command I give you: Love one another.

As I have loved you, so you must love one another. By this everyone will know that you are my disciples, if you love one another." Jesus gave the world the ultimate example of love through His death on the cross.

At times it is hard to see the love of God lived out in the lives of people who claim to be Jesus' disciples. We've seen hypocrisy, self-justification, hatred, and rejection by those who claim to be followers of Jesus. Imagine what the world would be like if every Christian lived like a Christian and loved people with God's love. Our world would be a very different place.

> Christians don't have to agree with people's behavior or beliefs to love and care for them.

At this point I have to address an important issue, and in reality it is a disclaimer. As you read what I'm writing, you may be saying to yourself, "This doesn't sound like the Christianity I often see on television. These ministries are often the subject of scandal, make millions from naïve followers, and 'ask for money' as their primary message."

To be sure, there are some excellent ministries and Bible teaching available on Christian television, but much of what you see does not reflect the values of Jesus or the God of the Bible. I apologize to you and ask you to look beyond some public examples and examine the Jesus of the New Testament.

What I can promise you is that lives are changed when the Word of God works in people's hearts. Jesus showed mercy, forgiveness, and acceptance to Paul and transformed him from a murderer into an agent of God's love. This is what the apostle Paul said about God's transforming work in his life:

> I thank Christ Jesus our Lord, who has given me strength, that he considered me trustworthy, appointing me to his service. Even though I was once a blasphemer and a persecutor and a violent man, I was shown mercy because I acted in ignorance and unbelief. The grace of our Lord was poured out on me abundantly, along with the faith and love that are in Christ Jesus.
>
> Here is a trustworthy saying that deserves full acceptance: Christ Jesus came into the world to save sinners—of whom I am the worst. But for that very reason I was shown mercy so that in me, the worst of sinners, Christ Jesus might display his immense patience as an example for those who would believe in him and receive eternal life. (1 Tim. 1:12–16)

God's truth is absolute and works for Christians and non-Christians alike. Raising kids is hard work, and God's Word provides effective guidelines to help parents on this journey. To help with the growing problem of juvenile delinquency in South Africa, a police department was looking for parenting materials to help parents as a preventative measure. They had no religious orientation, but they wanted something that would work. Over a period of two to three years, the South African police department handed out a book and small group DVD training nationwide that I had the privilege to author, called *Effective Parenting in a Defective World*. The biblical resources that taught parents, police, and youth how to treat one another had a significant and positive impact on their problem. In like manner, Prison Fellowship, a Christian organization started by Chuck Colson, has been given the opportunity to take over entire cell blocks in state prisons for prisoners who are willing to adhere to the Christian principles and Bible studies instituted in the volunteer environments. The results have been nothing short of dramatic with regard to violence, gangs, rehabilitation, and recidivism. The teaching of Jesus works!

Reason #6: The Evidence of Uniqueness

The evidence of uniqueness is the sixth reason I believe in the God of the Bible. God's chief messenger, Jesus, and the message of "grace," stand in contrast to all religions and religious practices. I believe this to be the strongest evidence of all.

Jesus is unique. He's not a prophet or just another teacher. Jesus is the Son of God and the only way to a relationship with God.

> In the beginning was the Word, and the Word was with God, and the Word was God. He was with God in the beginning. Through him all things were made; without him nothing was made that has been made. (John 1:1–3)

> The Word became flesh and made his dwelling among us. We have seen his glory, the glory of the one and only Son, who came from the Father, full of grace and truth. . . . For the law was given through Moses; grace and truth came through Jesus Christ. (John 1:14, 17)

Jesus is completely unique from all other religious messengers or truth claims. Jesus is sinless (John 12). Jesus is the Creator (Col. 1:16). Jesus is the Savior (Acts 4:12). Jesus claimed that He would build His church and the gates of hell would not prevail against it (Matt. 16:18). The church will move forward, invade evil, free people, and bring light to the world.

Jesus' message was as unique as His personhood. His message was a message of grace, and it is in complete contrast to all other religions. Grace is the unconditional, unmerited love of God toward every human being that compels Him to forgive and to reconcile them to Himself (all who are willing), based solely on the work of Christ on the cross. Religious performance and righteous works do not earn salvation or good standing with God.

> Only one God offers salvation absolutely free through His sacrifice on our behalf, and that is the God of the Bible.

In contrast to grace, human performance is at the foundation of every other world religion. Their message is work harder, follow this path, climb this ladder, obey these rules, appease a god, or attain enlightenment by the extent of your efforts.

Only one God offers salvation absolutely free through His sacrifice on our behalf, and that is the God of the Bible. There is nothing you can do to earn salvation. Salvation is by grace, and it is a gift that, when received, truly transforms you. The transformation is not from the outside in, trying to earn God's favor, but from the inside out. Jesus' message stands apart from all others.

For it is by grace you have been saved, through faith—and this is not from yourselves, it is the gift of God—not by works, so that no one can boast. (Eph. 2:8–9)

I am a visual person, and sometimes a picture helps me understand ideas. This picture helps me understand grace. I want you to imagine a long rack of bowling balls. Do you have the picture?

On one side of every bowling ball I want you to mentally write the name of a religion in big, bold lettering. You can put Islam, Buddhism, Hinduism, Shintoism, Taoism, or whatever religion you can think of. Then under the name in very small print visualize all the claims, rules, customs, and beliefs that this religion requires.

As you grab each bowling ball off the rack, you turn it over to reveal that each of the religious faiths are labeled with a two-letter summary: DO. What you are to do is different for each bowling ball, but the summary is the same. Then you get to one that is labeled "Christianity" with the name of Jesus on it. Inside are all the teachings of Jesus, fulfillment of prophecy, and everything we've talked about. As you turn it over to view its summary, you read the word DONE. That's the difference.

Christianity alone makes the claim that what a person needs most—forgiveness, love, acceptance, a new start, power to live above destructive behaviors—is a gift waiting to be opened and received. Christianity is not intolerant. It is narrow and true. What you could never do for yourself, Jesus did.

> We all, like sheep, have gone astray,
>   each of us has turned to our own way;
> and the LORD has laid on him
>   the iniquity of us all. (Isa. 53:6)

201

When we embrace the word DONE, we can live out of grace, as a dearly loved child. A child who could never earn His favor but one who already has it to the fullest because of Jesus' death and resurrection to pay for our sin and break its power in our lives.

Reason #7: The Existential Evidence

The millions of changed lives in the last two thousand years argue, experientially, that Jesus is alive, and is who He says He is.

There is something very powerful about a personal testimony. Even in Jesus' day we hear of a man born blind who was given his sight by Jesus (John 9). The religious leaders could not deny the miracle and twice interviewed the man to authenticate and get to the bottom of his story. When he was challenged to denounce Jesus as a sinner, his explanation was very simple: "Whether he is a sinner or not, I don't know. One thing I do know. I was blind but now I see!" (John 9:25).

Quite honestly, that was my story as well. Jesus has changed me from a driven, insecure, performance-oriented, egocentric man from an alcoholic family to a husband, father, and pastor who unexplainably (apart from God's grace) has become, on most days, a kind and others-centered follower of Christ.

My story reminds me of a famous old hymn written by John Newton, a man whose life was forever changed from a slave trader to a pastor seeking to abolish slavery through his relationship with Jesus. Read the lyrics to his song and let their message sink into your heart.

Amazing Grace

Amazing grace, how sweet the sound
That saved a wretch like me.
I once was lost but now I'm found.
Was blind, but now I see.

'Twas grace that taught my heart to fear
And grace my fears relieved.
How precious did that grace appear
The hour I first believed.

When we've been there ten thousand years,
Bright shining as the sun.
We've no less days to sing God's praise
Than when we first begun.

At some moment in time, experientially, Christians realize, "I was lost, but now I'm found. I was blind, and now I see." There is peace, forgiveness, joy, significance, love, and purpose in life. A new spiritual reality becomes normal.

Summary: So Why Don't People Believe?

We often have some mistaken assumptions when it comes to belief. We think that spiritual birth and spiritual understanding are intellectual issues alone. People may agree that evidence for the God of the Bible is logical and convincing, yet not believe it. Why?

After I preached a sermon on the resurrection and how to become a Christian, a man came up to me after the service and excitedly shared that this was exactly the information his dad needed to hear. He said, "My dad is very logical and that was so clear and the evidence so compelling that I'm sure my dad will believe after hearing that sermon." He had been praying for his dad for thirty-two years.

I saw him the next week and I asked, "Well, how's it going?" He said, "Oh man, such a bummer." I asked, "What do you mean?" He said, "Do you realize my dad sat in that service and listened to every word you said?" "Yeah, you told me he did." He replied, "Well, do you know what we talked about on the way home?" I asked, "What?" He answered, "Kentucky Fried Chicken. He just heard the gospel as clear as I've ever heard in my life and all he wanted to talk about was lunch."

> Belief is not purely an intellectual issue.

Belief is not purely an intellectual issue. Saving faith or belief have three formidable challenges. I want to share with you the three most common reasons why people do not place their faith in Christ and follow Him.

1. Ignorance

Most Christians, even those who regularly attend church across America, think that a relationship with Jesus requires them to "do" certain things to gain His approval. I grew up in church, but I was eighteen years old before I heard the gospel. All I got out of my negative religious experience was do, do, do, by a group of people who didn't even do what they were telling me to do. My response was, no thank you.

But the Bible says,

How can they call on the one they have not believed in? And how can they believe in the one of whom they have not heard? And how can they hear without someone preaching to them? And how can they preach unless they are sent? As it is written: "How beautiful are the feet of those who bring good news!" (Rom. 10:14–15)

We assume many people understand what Christianity really is, but they don't. They don't hear "Done"; all they hear is "Do." People think you want to recruit them into your church or religious system, instead of introducing them to a personal relationship with the living God that He has made available by GRACE!

2. Pride

The second reason people say no is pride. We are unwilling to admit our need. At the core of pride is control. We do not want to admit our need for God and receive His free gift of grace. We want to keep complete control of our lives for ourselves. There is a fear of what other people might think and what giving up control to God will cost us.

I was one of those people who thought Christianity was for weak people who needed a crutch. I was taught to be strong, to never show weakness, to set goals, work hard, and prove myself to the world. The idea of a "free gift" and me "needing help" were foreign to my thinking.

Ironically, it was the external success that came from my "self-made man" mantra that brought me to the end of myself. My success in sports, school, and with girls left me empty and questioning the meaning of life. Nevertheless, the thought of giving up control and of asking for help was extraordinarily difficult.

This was true in Jesus' day, just as it is today. The Gospel of John tells us that many people, even among the leaders, believed in Jesus but would not openly acknowledge their faith. They feared that they would be put out of the synagogue. They valued praise from their peers more than praise from God (John 12:42).

This is why Jesus said, "Unless you change and become like little children, you will never enter the kingdom of heaven" (Matt. 18:3). Little kids understand. They accept things at face value. When I say to my grandkids, "Let's go for ice cream," they cheer and jump in the car. They don't question what it will cost them or if I'll keep my promise. Children recognize their need and willingly accept the kindness of their parents.

The God of the universe asks us, "Would you like to be a part of My family? Would you like to be forgiven? Would you like to understand your purpose?" In response, we often react with fear of losing control and demand to know all the details. "Where am I going to sit in the car? What kind of ice cream are we going to have and who gets to pick it out?"

Additionally, pride at times manifests itself in our lives as we ponder the response of our closest relationships. "What would my wife really think?" or "What would my husband think?" or "What would the guys at work say?"

In the final analysis, what others think will not matter; but it requires genuine humility to admit our need, ask for forgiveness, and follow Jesus in the path of discipleship.

3. A Moral Problem

Sometimes the issue is neither ignorance nor pride. Our passions often overrule all logic and evidence about what is true.

I vividly remember doing an evangelistic Gospel of John Bible study with a group of college athletes. We would play pickup basketball, then head up to one of the dorm rooms and sit on the floor and read a chapter of the Gospel of John each week. There was no preaching or telling people what to do or what to believe. We read it out loud together and I asked questions about the passage so these young men could discover who Jesus claimed to be and what He offered to them in the world.

We built great relationships, often went out afterward to get a bite to eat, and just had fun together. After the fourth study, one of the young basketball players came to me and explained that he would not be attending any longer. I asked him why, and his response was both honest and revealing. He said plainly, "I can see where this is going. If I keep reading this and learning about Jesus, I'm going to have to make a decision about my lifestyle. I'm sleeping with my girlfriend, and I know if I put my faith in Christ, that will be something I need to change. I'm not giving up sex for Jesus."

We talked at length to make sure he understood how to receive the gift of eternal life should he ever decide to in the future. He actually shared the gospel with me so I knew that he fully understood it. I told him I sure hoped he would continue to play basketball with us, and that I would be available to talk whenever he wanted to in the future. He was a great guy and it broke my heart to see him exchange the gift of eternal life for second-rate sex. I say second-rate, because after working with college students for over a decade, I had seen the fallout, the guilt, the broken hearts, and the shame that sex outside of marriage continues to produce.

For others, it's a drug addiction, or a power trip from a position or job: but in the end it's a moral problem. It's not that they think there is no real evidence, or that the evidence is not convincing. Jesus summarizes this universal problem of our human bent toward the love of darkness instead of the light. John 3:19–20 says,

> This is the verdict: Light has come into the world, but people loved darkness instead of light because their deeds were evil. Everyone who does evil hates the light, and will not come into the light for fear that their deeds will be exposed.

At the end of the day, the reason many do not believe has nothing to do with the evidence. It is a moral problem that keeps them from receiving the light and the love of God.

Well, thanks for joining me on this journey of Why I Believe. For those who need more evidence or have questions about a particular topic, I have listed some great resources that have helped me along the way.

My prayer for you is that you will live your faith boldly and courageously. I pray you might realize afresh that your faith is not only intellectually feasible and grounded in history, but that it has shaped the world for good when sincerely and honestly applied. My prayer is that you will be a difference maker in your world. That you would live such a winsome, loving, and holy life that many will ask you about the hope within you . . . and now you will be able to explain it to them a little bit better.

––––––

Resources for Further Study:

C. S. Lewis, *The Problem of Pain*
Philip Yancey, *Where Is God When It Hurts?*
Tim Keller, *The Reason for God*
Nabeel Qureshi, *Seeking Allah, Finding Jesus*
Dean Halverson, *The Compact Guide to World Religions*
Dinesh D'Souza, *What's So Great about Christianity*
Rodney Stark, *The Rise of Christianity*
Rodney Stark, *The Triumph of Christianity*

Conclusion

I hope our journey together has been an encouragement to you. I hope you've taken the time to ask some of those penetrating questions about what you believe and why. I also hope this book will be a resource that you can share with friends and family who don't understand how you can be a Christian and be a thinking person.

Throughout our journey together we have examined the foundations of truth. As we close our walk along this path together, I would like you to imagine the truth of Jesus and all His claims as a BRIDGE that connects God on one side and people like you and me on the other. We have established that the bridge is trustworthy, but it is only through faith that we can cross the bridge to receive the gift of eternal life.

For years I somehow thought of eternal life as something that happens after I die. But as we discovered together, eternal life is not only about length of days, but also a completely new life and quality of life in Christ that begins the moment we put our faith in Him.

I've spent a lot of time talking directly to your head, by giving you the reasons why I didn't have to throw my brains in the trash to be a follower of Jesus. But I want to remind you that a relationship with God is fundamentally about the heart. God loves you and wants to be your Father, your Friend, and your Savior. When Jesus was asked what life is all about and what was the most important commandment, He stated clearly,

> Love the Lord your God with all your heart and with all your soul and with all your mind. This is the first and greatest commandment. And the second is like it: "Love your neighbor as yourself." (Matt. 22:37–39)

My prayer as we close our time together is that God will continue to strengthen your faith with the overwhelming evidence He has provided, so that your heart might become more and more drawn to Him and you will enjoy the amazing life He has for you.

Let's commit to be Christians who live like Christians, through the power of the Holy Spirit, every moment of every day. May we boldly share with others Why We Believe!

Selected Bibliography

Denis Alexander, *Creation or Evolution*

Kenneth D. Boa and Robert M. Bowman Jr., *Faith Has Its Reasons: An Integrating Approach to Defending Christianity*

Kenneth Boa and Larry Moody, *I'm Glad You Asked*

Dinesh D'Souza, *What's So Great about Christianity*

Dinesh D'Souza, *Life after Death*

Norman Geisler and Thomas Howe, *When Critics Ask*

Duane T. Gish, *Evolution: The Challenge of the Fossil Record*

Gary R. Habermas and J. P. Moreland, *Immortality: The Other Side of Death*

Hank Hanegraaff, *The Face That Demonstrates the Farce of Evolution*

Philip E. Johnson, *Darwin on Trial*

Philip E. Johnson, *Defeating Darwinism by Opening Minds*

Philip E. Johnson, *Reason in the Balance*

Lane P. Lester and Raymond G. Bolin, *The Natural Limits to Biological Change*

Paul E. Little, *Know Why You Believe*

Josh McDowell, *Evidence That Demands a Verdict*

Josh McDowell and Don Stewart, *Answers to Tough Questions Skeptics Ask about the Christian Faith*

Josh McDowell and Don Stewart, *Reasons Skeptics Should Consider Christianity*

Henry M. Morris, *The Biblical Basis for Modern Science*

Henry M. Morris and Gary E. Parker, *What Is Creation Science?*

Hugh Ross, *The Fingerprint of God*

Lee Strobel, *The Case for a Creator*

A. E. Wilder-Smith, Man's Origin, *Man's Destiny*

Notes

Chapter 1 Why I Believe in the Resurrection

1. Gary Habermas, Antony Flew, and Terry Miethe, *Did Jesus Rise from the Dead? The Resurrection Debate* (Eugene, OR: Wipf and Stock, 1987), 3.
2. Isaiah 7:14.
3. Isaiah 35:5–6.
4. Isaiah 7:14.
5. Micah 5:2.
6. Psalm 2:7.
7. Psalm 110:1.
8. Psalm 22.

Chapter 2 Did Jesus Really Die?

1. Will Durant, *Caesar and Christ*, vol. 3, *The Story of Civilization* (New York: Simon & Schuster, 2011).
2. Simon Greenleaf, *The Testimony of the Evangelists* (Grand Rapids: Kregel Classics, 1995), 41.
3. Sir Lionel Luckhoo, *What Is Your Verdict?* (N.P.: Fellowship Press, 1984), 12, cited in Ross Clifford, *Leading Lawyers Look at the Resurrection* (Claremont, CA: Albatross, 1991), 112; https://www.jashow.org/articles/general/the-truth-about-the-founder-of-christianitypart-6/#cite_note-3.

Chapter 3 Why I Believe in the Bible

1. Edwin W. Lutzer, *Seven Reasons Why You Can Trust the Bible* (Chicago: Moody, 1998).
2. Bill Wilson, *The Best of Josh McDowell: A Ready Defense* (Nashville: Thomas Nelson, 1993).

3. "The Tel Dan Inscription: The First Historical Evidence of King David from the Bible," Bible History Daily, *Biblical Archaeology*, Nov. 8, 2016, http://www.biblicalarchaeology.org/daily/biblical-artifacts/artifacts-and-the-bible/the-tel-dan-inscription-the-first-historical-evidence-of-the-king-david-bible-story/.

4. William M. Ramsay, *The Bearing of Recent Discovery on the Trustworthiness of the New Testament* (London: Hodder and Stoughton, 1915), 222.

5. Nelson Glueck, *Rivers in the Desert: A History of the Negev* (New York: Farrar, Straus and Cudahy, 1959), 31.

6. Terry Hall, "How We Got Our Old Testament," *Moody Monthly Journal*, January 1987, 32.

7. Rene Pache, *The Inspiration and Authority of Scripture* (Chicago: Moody, 1969), 215–21.

8. Charles Caldwell Ryrie, *What You Should Know about Inerrancy* (Chicago: Moody, 1981), 58–63.

Chapter 4 Don't Take My Word for It

1. Peter Stoner, *Science Speaks*, rev. ed. (Chicago: Moody, 1976).

2. Wilson, *The Best of Josh McDowell*.

Chapter 5 Why I Believe in Life after Death

1. C. S. Lewis, *Mere Christianity* (1952; repr., New York: HarperOne, 2001), 136–37.

2. Adam Withnall, "Life after Death? Largest-ever Study Provides Evidence That 'Out of Body' and 'Near-Death' Experiences May Be Real," Independent.co.uk, http://www.independent.co.uk/news/science/life-after-death-largest-ever-study-provides-evidence-that-out-of-body-and-near-death-experiences-9780195.html.

3. Sam Parnia et al., "AWARE—Awareness during Resuscitation—A Prospective Study," *Resuscitation* 85(12): 1799–1805.

4. "Life after Death," Anthropology, http://anthropology-world.blogspot.com/2013/11/life-after-death.html.

5. C. S. Lewis, *The Problem of Pain* (1944; repr., New York: HarperCollins, 2001), 128.

6. Ibid., 121.

Chapter 6 Why I Believe in Creation

1. "Poll: Americans Overwhelmingly Support the Right of Students, Teachers, and Scientists to Discuss Dissenting Scientific Views on Evolution," Discovery Institute, July 1, 2016, http://www.discovery.org/scripts/viewDB/filesDB-download.php?command=download&id=12049.

2. Duane Gish, "The Nature of Science and of Theories on Origins," *Acts & Facts* 24, no. 4 (1995).

3. L. C. Birch and P. R. Ehrlich, *Nature* 214 (1967): 349.

4. Carl Sagan, "The Best of *Cosmos*" broadcast, PBS.

5. Richard Dawkins, *The Blind Watchmaker: Why the Evidence Reveals a Universe Without Design* (New York: W. W. Norton, 1987), 317.

6. Jane J. Lee, "Why Bill Nye Calls Evolution 'Undeniable' and Creationism 'Inane,'" Book Talk, *National Geographic*, January 24, 2015, http://news.nationalgeographic.com/news/2015/01/150125-bill-nye-science-guy-evolution-creation-book-talk-culture/.

7. James F. Jekel, "The Mystery of Life's Origin: Reassessing Current Theories," Book Reviews, *Yale Journal of Biology and Medicine* 58, no. 4 (July–August 1985): 407–8.

8. Michael Denton, *Evolution: A Theory in Crisis* (Chevy Chase, MD: Adler and Adler, 1986).

9. Francis Crick, *Life Itself: Its Origin and Nature* (New York: Simon & Schuster, 1982).

10. Søren Løvtrup, *Darwinism: The Refutation of a Myth* (New York: Springer, 1987).

11. Craig Rusbult, PhD, "Evolution & the National Association of Biology Teachers: NABT claimed 'evolution was an unsupervised process,'" http://www.asa3.org/ASA/education/origins/nabt.htm.

Chapter 7 Science or God: The False Dichotomy

1. Charles Robert Darwin, *On the Origin of Species* (London: John Murray, 1859; ebook 2013), https://www.gutenberg.org/files/1228/1228-h/1228-h.htm.

2. Maulana Wahiduddin Khan, *God Arises: Evidence of God in Nature and in Science* (New Delhi, India: Goodword Books, 1985).

3. Spiros Zodhiates, "The Odds Are against Evolution," Pulpit Helps, *Disciple Magazine*, October 1996.

4. Francis Crick, *The Facts on Creation vs. Evolution* (Eugene, OR: Harvest House, 1993), 20.

5. Liza Gross, "Edwin Hubble: The Great Synthesizer Revealing the Breadth and Birth of the Universe," http://www.exploratorium.edu/origins/hubble/people/edwin.html.

6. "A Scientist Caught between Two Faiths: Interview with Robert Jastrow," *Christianity Today*, August 6, 1982.

7. Robert Jastrow, *God and the Astronomers* (Toronto: George J. McLeod Limited, 1994).

8. Darwin, *On the Origin of Species*.

9. L. Sunderland, *Darwin's Enigma* (Green Forest, AR: Master Books, 1998), 101–2. Patterson's letter was written in 1979.

10. Thomas Nagel, *The Last Word* (Oxford: Oxford University Press, 1997), 130–31.

11. Charles Darwin, letter to William Graham, July 3, 1881, Darwin Correspondence Project, University of Cambridge, https://www.darwinproject.ac.uk/letter/?docId=letters/DCP-LETT-13230.xml;query=Caucasian%20races%20have%20beaten%20the%20Turkish%20hollow;brand=default.

12. Thomas Huxley, *Lay Sermons, Addresses, and Reviews* (New York: Appleton, 1871), 20.

13. Charles Darwin, *The Descent of Man*, vol. 2 (New York: Appleton, 1871), 327.

14. Henry Morris, *Men of Science, Men of God* (Green Forest, AR: Master Books, 1982; rev. 1988).

15. Hank Hanegraaff, *The Face That Demonstrates the Farce of Evolution* (Nashville: Word Publishing, 1998).

16. Ibid.

17. Ibid.

18. Ibid.

19. Ibid.

Chapter 8 Why I Believe in the God of the Bible

1. "Major Religions of the World Ranked by Number of Adherents," Adherents.com, http://www.adherents.com/Religions_By_Adherents.html.

2. Siby K. Joseph, "Gandhi, Religion and Multiculturalism: An Appraisal," http://www.mkgandhi.org/articles/gandhi_religion.html.

3. Jim Romenesko, "Winners of Livingston Awards for Young Journalists Named," The Pointer Institute, Poynter.org, June 3, 2009, http://www.poynter.org/2009/winners-of-livingston-awards-for-young-journalists-named-3/96102/.

4. http://www.johnsdickerson.com/national-writing/.

5. See John S. Dickerson, *Jesus Skeptic* (Grand Rapids: Baker Books, forthcoming), unedited manuscript. John's extract is thoroughly researched and his endnotes for this material can be found in his book, which will be published in 2019.

Chip Ingram is the senior pastor of Venture Christian Church in Los Gatos, California, and teaching pastor and president of Living on the Edge, an international teaching and discipleship ministry. A pastor for over thirty years, Chip has a unique ability to communicate truth and challenge people to live out their faith. Chip is the author of many books, including *The Real God*, *Culture Shock*, *The Real Heaven*, *The Invisible War*, and *Love, Sex, and Lasting Relationships*. Chip and his wife, Theresa, have four grown children and eleven grandchildren and live in California.

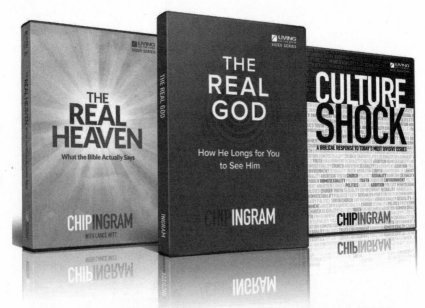

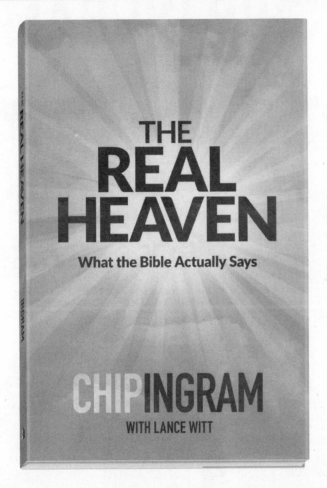

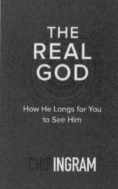
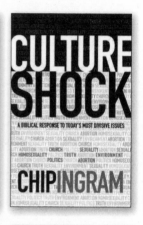